CAPTAIN'S LOG

CAPTAIN'S LOG
The Gary McAllister Story

Gary McAllister
with
Graham Clark

Best Wishes

[signature]

MAINSTREAM
PUBLISHING

EDINBURGH AND LONDON

First published in Great Britain in 1995 by
MAINSTREAM PUBLISHING COMPANY (EDINBURGH) LTD
7 Albany Street
Edinburgh EH1 3UG

ISBN 1 85158 790 X

A catalogue record for this book is available from the British Library

Every attempt has been made to contact the copyright holders of the
photographic material reproduced in this book. We apologise if, by being
unable to trace certain sources, we have unknowingly failed to
acknowledge copyright material

Typeset in 12 on 14 pt Bembo
Printed and bound in Great Britain by Butler & Tanner Ltd, Frome

Contents

CHAPTER ONE

Shattered Dreams

When you think of the fierce rivalry between Leeds United and Manchester United, it's almost sacrilege to admit that at one time I supported the Old Trafford club. But I did and, to be honest, it was almost an obsession with me when I was a youngster – an impressionable youngster, I hasten to add.

The only case I can make for my own defence is that I was born and brought up in Bellshill and my family was close to a family with a name that was – and still is – synonymous with Manchester United: Busby. Sir Matt, one of the truly great football people of the post-war era, came from the same corner of Lanarkshire, and I suppose that was part of the reason for my leaning towards Manchester United. But remember, too, that players like Bobby Charlton, Pat Crerand and Denis Law were all around at the same time and any youngster would have followed their fortunes. I certainly did, although it was difficult early on in life because my mum, Helen, and dad, Samuel, decided to emigrate to Canada when I was only two. That move, way back in 1966, must have been a huge adventure although there's obviously not much of it I can remember. And, anyway, it didn't last long because Mum wasn't too keen on Toronto and we were soon on the way back home, first to Mossend and then to New Stevenston, ultimately ending up at Newarthill. They are all fairly small places almost within a free kick of each other, but we were a family who liked our roots and we had all manner of relations around the area.

It was a comfortable upbringing for me, although when I was only eight I came to realise that everything in life doesn't always go the way you want. That was when Mum died, leaving Dad, my younger brother, Craig, and I on our own. It was a terrible shock, especially to Dad, and my clearest recollection of that period was the awful hurt he felt. He was badly affected at the time. Craig and I were still young and maybe it didn't have quite the same impact, although even now one of my biggest regrets in life is that I can't remember much about the woman who brought me into this world.

Mum's death meant Craig and I lived a lot with various aunties because, with Dad working full time, there was no real alternative. But we were well looked after and I have to say I can't remember ever wanting for much.

I was always, of course, interested in football and I seemed to be able to get boots and strips and all the things you need when you're a budding professional – or at least dreaming of becoming one! And when I became hooked on golf, which is altogether a more expensive pastime, I was given clubs and shoes. Basically, I was lucky.

I certainly enjoyed golf, though – I still do. But at the time I divided my 'talents' between that and football and, looking back on it now, I'm not at all sure how I fitted in school! Somehow I must have, but my only interests, for sure, were those two sports. And I must have been able to play in some shape or form. When I was fifteen I was a reserve for the Scotland golf side for a match at Gullane, and among the lads playing at around the same time were Lee Vannet and Adam Hunter, who have both gone on to do well in the sport.

But if I wasn't that keen on school, it's also true to say I wasn't entirely stupid, and I was quick enough, for instance, to realise that although I was handy at golf I was nowhere near good enough to earn a living from the game. It was a nice thought but dreams don't pay wages. And, really, football was undoubtedly my first love. I played at Keir Hardie Primary School in Newarthill and at Braidhurst High School in Motherwell, and when I was eleven I joined Fir Park Boys Club. The Motherwell team of the time – the Boys Club was linked to 'Well – included players like Bobby Graham and Joe Wark, whom I thought were tremendous. And there was a lad there called Vic Davidson who many people reckoned would go on to become the new Kenny Dalglish. Vic wore the number 10 jersey, as did Denis Law at Manchester United, and I think those two early favourites left me with a bit of a fixation for that number that has stayed with me all through my career. I was at the age when all sorts of people influenced me in a big way.

The guys at the Boys Club like Norrie Cranston, Bobby French and Alex Foster were a big help to all the youngsters starting out on the long and difficult road. They taught me, and others, all the good things that stay with you throughout your life in the game. Joe Wark, too, was a massive help because he did a lot of coaching at the time and he preached good things and put sound ideas into practice. He advocated seven-a-side games for younger lads, for instance, and that's the kind of thing currently being actively encouraged all over the country. He just had a lot of fundamentally good habits which struck a chord with me and, hopefully, I've tried to maintain the standards all these people encouraged.

I was also fortunate to be able to go with the Boys Club to youth tournaments in places like Holland, Belgium and even the United States, and those trips broadened my horizons in terms of life and football. It was all invaluable experience. But the one thing it didn't prepare me for was the heartbreak to follow.

Motherwell wanted me to sign for them when I was just twelve, but when your bedroom is full of Manchester United posters and paraphernalia, it's not easy to change your affections from red to claret and amber. That's why when Manchester United showed an interest I went running south. Maybe it was the Busby connection that encouraged them to invite me down, or maybe it was just because I showed a little bit of promise. Whatever the reason, I couldn't get down to Manchester quick enough. And, when I did, the first people I bumped into were youngsters, lads of my age, in the shape of Norman Whiteside, Mark Hughes and Graeme Hogg. We were all there for a summer stint and stayed at United's hall of residence. It was the same story for the following three summers when we would all appear and love every second of our involvement.

I had always wanted to play in England – for United – so it was shaping up nicely to be a dream come true. Manchester City – perish the thought – Newcastle United and Nottingham Forest were all showing a bit of interest as well, but it wasn't reciprocated. There was only one club for me.

Dave Sexton was United manager at the time and Syd Owen was in charge of us youngsters. Big names like Joe Jordan, Gordon McQueen, Lou Macari and Ray Wilkins were around the place. I was in heaven!

One year, around the start of the season, United held an open day and an international five-a-side tournament was set up among the professionals. There was an England team, an Irish side, an international mix and, naturally, a Scottish select. But one of the Scots failed to turn up and I was drafted into a side that included people like McQueen and Martin Buchan – and I was only thirteen. What an experience that was.

Yet when the crunch came and there was talk of an offer from United, I decided, instead of signing, to sit my O-levels. Don't ask me why I did that. I think I was following the usual advice directed at youngsters to make sure I had qualifications behind me and so on. Whatever the reason, I missed my chance.

Ron Atkinson duly replaced Sexton as manager and I was told pretty soon after that that I wasn't being taken on. It was hard to take because by then I was ready, willing and apparently able. In fact, it was more than hard to take. I was devastated. I had told all the other interested clubs that I wanted to play for

United and no one else. Stan Anderson, for example, had invited me to join Rangers but my heart was set on Old Trafford. So, when I was dumped, it was much more than simply hard to take. When I discovered I wasn't going to fulfil that dream I flew upstairs to my bedroom and tore up and got rid of all the United stuff I had collected. It was all a bit sore.

No one ever really did explain why I wasn't being signed, and to this day lads like Hughes and Whiteside can't quite understand why I failed to appear back at the club thereafter. I often wonder myself how things would have worked out but, of course, there's no way of telling. I look back on that awful moment now and realise I was taught a harsh lesson. It was pretty desperate at the time but I think it toughened me up in the long term.

Other clubs were still interested – including Leeds – but since I had put all my eggs in one basket earlier, I didn't really think it was the right thing to do to go back to any of them. And I knew Motherwell had always wanted me throughout my association with the Boys Club.

So, in 1980, when I was sixteen, I joined the 'Well ground staff where a guy called Andy Russell became my first proper boss. Did I say proper? Andy is as much of a legend – well, he likes to think so – around Fir Park now as he was then. And he made sure there was never any slacking from myself and the only other apprentice, a lad called Junior Burns. We did every conceivable job around Fir Park, from cleaning the boots of the twenty-five professionals at the time to painting the ground and cutting the grass. It was hard work but it was a step in the right direction. And we had some laughs.

The club had an Alsatian for a guard dog and one of my jobs was to feed the beast. Now, it wasn't the friendliest of animals although I got along fine with it because I was the provider of its meals. But I was privileged, because it certainly wasn't too keen on anyone else. One bitterly cold winter's day, when I was all wrapped up ready to go out and sweep the terraces, I was trying to prepare myself for the elements by huddling next to the big boiler where all the kit was dried. It was the cosiest room at Fir Park and a few people had gathered round the boiler for some heat. Then, from nowhere, this great big Alsatian appeared at the door and I can honestly say I've never seen some of those people move as quickly. Well, that's not quite accurate, because when they all tried to escape by climbing on to this boiler, they moved even faster then because it was red hot! It was a memorable scene.

But it was all basically good fun for Junior and me and, most importantly of all, it was a step on the first rung of the ladder. And, for me, after the massive disappointment of Manchester United, it was a huge step. Even though Motherwell was just down the road from home, it seemed to me that I had gone a long way to get there.

Looking back on it now, I suppose it was the perfect move for me in many ways. I was close to the family rather than being stranded hundreds of miles away in Manchester, and that was quite important. The McAllisters have always been a fairly close-knit family and, certainly, the Bellshill–Newarthill–Motherwell area where we and the Busbys live is quite a community. Even now the families are close, and when Sir Matt passed away I went to the funeral not as a footballer but to represent the McAllister family. I think Sir Matt was proud of what I had managed to achieve. Mind you I don't really think I've ever forgiven the club he loved so much.

CHAPTER TWO

'Well on the Way

The hurt of rejection eases over the course of time and the pain of being abandoned by Manchester United lessened slightly when I began to make my presence felt at Motherwell. In my years at Fir Park I think I learned a lot. Some of it was good, some of it bad and some of it indifferent, but invariably it was interesting.

Look at my managers for a start. There was Davie Hay, then Jock Wallace, followed by Bobby Watson and finally Tommy McLean. I don't think any of them fitted into any particular managerial mould – or, if they did, it must have been broken after they were all made! Davie actually made me his first signing and I shall be forever grateful to him for that. And at the time I was fortunate that all Davie's players – first team, reserves and kids – all trained together so I was involved from the start.

I got £300 to sign and then £40 a week and, considering I was still a teenager at the time and living at home with no rent to pay, it was like winning the lottery. I remember wondering what I would do with that amount of money every week although, equally, I can't recall any great problem spending it.

The other beauty – money apart – about signing for a club like Motherwell is that you always have a chance of making the breakthrough quickly. I know Manchester United have a reputation for bringing on kids but homely Fir Park offers an even faster route into first-team action than Old Trafford. And so it proved. I went more or less straight into the reserves and it didn't take me long to discover the facts of football life. There was I, a fresh-faced youth, in against some of the top players in the country almost before I had found my feet. Second-team football is partly made up of experienced professionals who have either been dropped or been injured. Either way, they generally have a point to prove. And not many are about to let a new kid on the block forget that.

Jim McSherry of Ayr United was a classic case in point. Motherwell faced Ayr in one of my first games for the second string and the bold Jim wasted no time in introducing me to the serious side of the game. He actually stood on me just to confirm he was around and, let me tell you, it was a bit of a shock to the system. There wasn't too much of that at Boys Club level and for all the world it seemed to me like a wee reminder that I was in among the big boys now.

But a big boy I certainly wasn't. I was, on the contrary, a midget, and even though I'm just about six foot tall now, all my pals from those days still call me 'Wee Man'. In fact, I grew from around five foot four inches to about six foot in a year. From being too small for the Under-18 Schoolboys side, I suddenly grew up – literally.

But the tiny McAllister bumped into some more big 'uns before he sprouted, and I remember coming up against Rangers' Colin McAdam in one game and thinking he was some sort of Colossus. Alan McInally, who went on to play for Celtic, Aston Villa and Bayern Munich, was another who seemed awfully big at the time. But I survived those clashes – somehow – and with guys like Brian McClair doing the business for the first team, we were on course for the old First Division title by Christmas.

That's maybe why when Davie Hay took the squad away to Portugal for a few days after the turn of the year he took Junior Burns and me with them. We got a fair bit of stick, naturally, from the other lads but we enjoyed the experience. We had a few good laughs over there, and we were even invited out by the senior lads on the last night. I survived that somehow as well!

Things went so smoothly on the field that Davie even allowed me the luxury of a first-team game at the end of the season. It was, as I remember, against Queen of the South at Palmerston and, when the score reached 4–0, Davie must have thought I wouldn't be too much of a gamble. In the end, we wɔn by six and I had had my first genuine taste of the big time.

But even in those heady days I was still turning out for the youth team, and one guy I came up against regularly was a youngster called Paul McStay. Paul and I were head-to-head a lot then, but one of us was in the headlines at the time and it wasn't me. He was – *is* – a tremendous player and around that time he was captain of the Scotland Under-21 side and, I think, had even played for the senior international team. I was a novice in comparison, and although we regularly competed against each other, I was way behind in terms of representative honours and therefore, I suppose, ability.

But I wasn't too unhappy with my progress and even the departure of Hay for Celtic and the arrival of Jock Wallace didn't unduly interrupt proceedings. But it would be difficult to imagine a greater contrast to laid-back Davie than man-mountain Jock. If I thought Colin McAdam was a Colossus, he was nothing compared to Wallace. That was like comparing David to Goliath. Jock was a very intimidating figure for a relatively raw recruit and, for that matter, for the most senior and experienced professionals. The man who bossed Rangers twice in a glittering managerial career was a frightening sight in full flight, and Jock seemed to be in full flight at regular intervals.

But for all his awesome size and seemingly invincible aura, Jock was terrific with me. He and his assistant, Frank Connor, immediately set about starting up a proper youth scheme so that there were more than just a couple of young players around the club. And he always took an interest in the players who weren't fixtures in and around the first team.

He picked me up once – quite literally by the scruff of the neck – and told me I would eventually play for Scotland. He really wanted us to do well – he willed it even – and the younger lads loved him for that. He was desperate to make sure anyone with even a modicum of talent didn't waste it. He just wanted everyone to achieve what they were capable of, and there's nothing wrong with that. It was a new approach to the youngsters and although it might not have been new to some of the older lads, it was certainly novel.

Big Jock knew a thing or two about the game and had proved it by leading Rangers to trebles and also doing well at Leicester City before he arrived at Fir Park. He had, in short, seen and done it all. Or so it seemed. What he presumably hadn't come across before was Andy Ritchie. Wallace, though, decided to sign the man who was, essentially, a Scottish Glenn Hoddle although what they shared was sheer ability rather than Glenn's economy of movement. Andy made Hoddle look like Mr Perpetual Motion. So it was a strange signing in view of Jock's penchant for hard work and Andy's positive hatred of same. But the manager clearly felt he could change the habits of a lifetime and set about the task with some gusto.

We went up to Dingwall to play Ross County on one occasion and you had to cross a bridge to get to the pitch. We were all in blazers, shirts and ties, etc, when all of a sudden we saw Jock pull Andy to the side and go down to a field which had more cow dung than grass in it. The next thing we saw is Ritchie getting his kit off and being ordered to do sit-ups in the middle of the field! Jock never was over-impressed with Andy's fitness.

As it happened, I didn't feature much in the first team during Wallace's reign but I still learned a lot from him because you simply couldn't ignore what he had achieved in all his years in the game. When he eventually left for a second stint at his beloved Rangers, I was sorry to see him go.

Jock was replaced by Bobby Watson who, in his spare time,

was a lay preacher. But the move never really worked out and although, ironically, I was in the team more than before, not a lot went right and the club went into serious decline. For example, we played at St Johnstone once and the pitch was covered in six inches of mud. Ideal conditions for me! But when we got to half-time we could hardly recognise each other. It was ridiculous. And it became even more ridiculous when, during the interval, the lads were looking for fresh kit and there wasn't any. We had to go back out the way we were. Although it was a relatively minor incident, it shows just how far downhill the club had gone. It was certainly the lowest point in my time at Fir Park.

So, when Watson left and was replaced by Tommy McLean, maybe the club could go only one way – and that was up. The former Rangers star saved us from relegation to the old Second Division – and who knows what would have happened to Motherwell if we had gone down – and the following season took us up to the top flight.

Wee Tam arrived at Fir Park after a useful stint with Morton although he had also been assistant manager to John Greig at Rangers before that. He had been a tremendous player, too, and not all that many years ago, so he was on the right wavelength with the players for a start. He actually went through the place like a tornado and freshened everything up from top to bottom. His training was probably the best organised I have ever experienced because he knew exactly what he wanted to do every day and who he wanted to do it with. There was nothing haphazard about it and it was all pre-planned down to the finest detail.

I think, looking back on the period now, that he learned a lot from the Scottish Football Association's coaching courses at Largs, because I've seen at first hand similar planning from other people who have been part of what is often referred to as the 'Largs mafia'. But it worked a treat for us. We survived that first season and were by far the best team in the division the next.

Motherwell had some good players then and guys like Andy Dornan, Andy Harrow and my wee pal, Ali Mauchlen, were all brought in. It was a decent squad and we were well led by McLean.

The wee man had a habit of appearing to be nagging you from the moment you walked into Fir Park till the moment you went out again after training. But I think he had the players' interests at heart and I've discovered since that when a manager stops nagging you and shouting at you and generally making your life occasionally fairly miserable, then he's lost interest. And that's when you know you're in trouble. You could never accuse Tam of that. I certainly couldn't, because he tended to protect me at the time. I was still fairly new to it all and he deliberately played me out wide where I could get more time, rather than in the middle of midfield where it all got a bit hot. He also took me to one side regularly and gave me the benefit of sound advice.

So in the 1984–85 season everything went pretty well. We were going well in the League and even had time for a good Scottish Cup run. We actually reached the semis, where we met Celtic, but there was a moment on that run to Hampden when the old adage 'once a Ranger, always a Ranger' was shown to be true as far as Tommy was concerned. We were on our way to the national stadium for that clash with Celtic when a famous song associated with Ibrox came over the coach sound-system. It certainly had the desired effect on a few of the lads though one or two others didn't look quite so happy because, in Scotland, a lot of players are brought up to support one or other of the Old Firm.

It was at that same game that I realised just what a terrific support Motherwell had – although where some of the fans went the rest of the season I'm not sure. They turned out that day, though, and they were rewarded with a 1–1 draw with the 'Well goal coming courtesy of G. McAllister Esq. In fact, we were unlucky not to win the game and as so often happens in games against either of Scotland's big two clubs you regret not winning first time round. Tommy Burns earned the Celts their draw and in the replay three late goals – two from Maurice Johnston and one from Roy Aitken – saw us off.

But promotion was fair consolation and the fact that I scored a few goals made it, all round, a good year for me. We actually won the First Division Championship at Forfar and at the end of it all I must have looked like a streaker because the supporters nicked most of my gear. But we had a good journey home after the match and those are the moments you enjoy remembering.

Ali Mauchlen and I had a good partnership going in that side after he had arrived from Kilmarnock, and it was a kind of Little and Large thing. He was Little but at the same time he was my minder. It just seemed to happen that way, and any time I was in bother he would appear at my side to sort it out. Equally, if *someone* needed sorting out, then Ali was my main man. But he was also an outstanding player and even in those early days he was a big influence on me. We didn't know it at the time but we would end up becoming a midfield partnership – and big pals – even after Fir Park.

The break with Motherwell wasn't all that long in coming after our title win. There was a fair bit of transfer speculation about Ali first and foremost, but also about me during that summer. So, by the time we came to open the season on Lanarkshire Cup duty at Hamilton, the Douglas Park stand had more scouts and managers in it than fans. One man who didn't sit and watch the action was the Leicester City boss, Gordon Milne. For some reason he stood behind the goal to see us win the Cup but he must have seen enough from there to be impressed and afterwards Tommy McLean pulled Ali and me aside and told us of the Filbert Street side's interest. Things snowballed from there and, to be honest, that was the end as far as our Motherwell careers were concerned.

Wee Tam had long known about my desire to go down south and try my luck against the Hoddles and Wilkinses of the world, and Ali was no different. We were more or less committed to Leicester before we played in the opening game of the season against Clydebank, and I think both of us felt we had signed the deal of a lifetime. It probably wasn't that great but we were well pleased. And Motherwell pocketed £250,000 for the pair of us, which at the time was understood to be £150,000 for Ali and the rest for me. Subsequently I discovered it was the other way round but I don't think the Fir Park club were too bothered about that minor detail.

And neither were we when we met the Bankies that day. We were desperate to be part of the team so we could show off the Championship trophy to the fans, but maybe it was a wee bit obvious that we were on our way. Clydebank star Gerry McCabe obviously smelled a rat because he kept asking where we were going! And, indeed, straight after that match we headed south for our medicals. They were no problem and lasted only half an hour or so each – which was just a bit different to the one I endured when I later left Filbert Street for Leeds United. It lasted eight-and-a-half hours!

But the main thing for me was that I was back in England where I had seemed destined to be much earlier in my career. And the prospect of mixing it with the best was a mouth-watering thought. I was particularly looking forward to facing Glenn Hoddle who was, as far as I was concerned, the greatest. I've mentioned before that I had a bit of a thing about the number 10 jersey and Glenn wore it more often than not. He was so naturally gifted and his movement, passing and awareness were brilliant. All that talk of his not being able to run and tackle was so much nonsense. There's more to football than being a long-distance athlete and having the ability to whack a fellow professional. Simply being talented is good enough for me, and although it's no skin off my nose, I would say that Hoddle never ever got the respect he deserved as a top-class player. He had so much natural flair that the game came easily to him – and that can't be said of all our players.

That's maybe what attracted me to that jersey because when you look around, some of the greatest players have all worn the number 10. Diego Maradona and Johan Cruyff are two, and I remember Tony Currie in England who was an outstanding talent in that position as well. There's not a lot wrong with basic ability.

CHAPTER THREE

In Among the Big Boys

I was glad to have Ali Mauchlen alongside me when we went to Leicester City because I'm not sure I would have stuck it out there if we hadn't been big pals. The reception we got at Filbert Street wasn't exactly overwhelming. A few of the City players had been there for a while and they clearly resented two newcomers coming down from Scotland to break up the side a bit. It was, to say the least, a bit difficult. It would have been hard enough for Ali and me to try and settle in a different city with a new team anyway without the problems we encountered with one or two of the players.

To be fair, it wasn't everyone, because there were Scots lads there like Bobby Smith and Ian Wilson, and when players from north of the border get together there generally aren't any problems.

But when you're a new face you want to be able to get on with all the lads, and that clearly wasn't the case at Leicester. We fell out with a few here and there and one day at training I got a nasty whack on the ankle from an experienced City pro who should have known better. It was a sore enough kick to get Ali – my minder – racing halfway across the Belvoir Drive training pitch to remonstrate with the offender.

The atmosphere really wasn't all that good and it was made pretty clear to us that the welcome mat wasn't going to be put down for our benefit. The upshot of that was that after a couple of days in Leicester Ali and I had had enough. We were ready to head home again. We hadn't necessarily expected the red-carpet treatment but, equally, we hadn't anticipated the way we had been received. You could actually *sense* the fact that we were interlopers.

But, as so often happens, it needed just one daft prank to ease the atmosphere a bit. We were staying at a place called Forest Lodge and I received a phone call one night from a football magazine reporter who asked me a variety of questions about my move from Motherwell. The interview lasted quite some time and I was happy enough to do it because, apart from anything else, I believe that dealing with the media is a fundamental part of the job. But in this instance, the 'media' man turned out to be my City teammate Bobby Smith, who promptly relayed the whole 'interview' – chapter and verse – to the rest of the lads. It helped to break the ice a bit, and although he probably didn't realise it, maybe Bobby's efforts helped Ali and I go on to make our careers in England.

We were accepted more and more as time went on, and our earlier trips home became less regular than they had at first, when we seemed to be bolting back across the border as often as possible.

The irony of that unhappy start was that we both liked Leicester itself and, for that matter, the club. We had doubled our wages going from Motherwell, which is always a good start, and considering we hadn't even been to the city to visit before we signed, we were pleasantly surprised by Leicester and its surroundings. There again, we had both been desperate to get to England, so we were probably a pushover for manager Milne when it came to cash.

And early on in my City career, the real reason why I had signed became very apparent. We were at Anfield to play Liverpool and the manager walked me out to the centre of the pitch there, waved his arm around and said: 'This is why you're here, to play at places like this.' And he was one hundred per cent right. Scottish grounds are fine but it's really only when you play for – or against – the Old Firm of Rangers and Celtic that you play in front of big crowds. That's what any player worth his salt wants to do *every* week, not just three or four times a season.

The other part of all that is that I wanted to find out how good – or bad – I was. I wanted to mix with the Kenny Dalglishes and Alan Hansens and all the rest of the big names up and down the country. The only way to prove yourself – sink or swim, if you like – is to go in among the big boys, and that's what I was anxious to do. And the chance for me came much earlier than I, or anyone else, had anticipated.

I made my debut against Ipswich Town and felt I did well in a draw but after that it was a bit of a rollercoaster season as so often seems to be the case at Filbert Street. We got a standing ovation at Anfield, won against Tottenham at White Hart Lane and competed brilliantly against the likes of Manchester United. Those games weren't the problem ones. Our difficulties were against the likes of Ipswich, Birmingham and Oxford. It was a bit frustrating but, as I say, City have made a history of that. At the end of the day we beat Newcastle United to stay in the top division, so it was all a bit fraught.

But I enjoyed it all. I loved the big-time atmosphere wherever we went and I was competing against all the players I had wanted to, which was an instant turn-on. And once things had settled down for Ali and me, we really enjoyed playing for City. Manager Gordon Milne signed Russell Osman from Ipswich and I got on well with him. It was good to have players of his calibre in the side – Russ had played for Town at the highest level and had also played for England. I listened to experienced men like him – and learned.

Alan Smith was another lad I liked, and although it will probably astonish many people, I would honestly say he is the best striker I have ever played behind. I have played with front men with more ability, but for a midfield man like me he was the perfect guy to have in front of you. Alan made so many unselfish runs and did so much hard work off the ball – as well as weighing in with a lot of goals – that it was a joy to be in the middle of the park. He made my life a bit easier because he was always trying to find space. And apart from all that, he introduced me to the serious business of drinking red wine!

Then there was Ian Andrews who became, unfairly, much maligned later in his career when he went to Celtic and in one match lost five goals to Rangers. The keeper was tremendous for Leicester and was probably *the* main reason for us staying up.

But when all the dust had settled, I felt I had done my bit as well considering it was my first season in England, and Ali, too, had been an influence. And that was despite he and his wife, Beth, and their children, Ian and Gillian, having me as a lodger.

There were changes at Filbert Street, though, and Bryan Hamilton became manager, with Peter Morris as his assistant. I seemed to be going through managers in jig time both at Leicester and Motherwell and, although I was a common denominator, I never took it personally. But when a club changes its manager, it is always an anxious time for a player. You never know whether or not the new boss will rate you or, come to that, if you will fancy him to do the job.

I didn't know Bryan at all other than knowing he had been a very good player for Northern Ireland, but I got on okay with him and, in fact, found some of his views quite refreshing. He had played a lot on Merseyside where they like to see their sides play football, and that was fine by me. But not everyone got on with the new boss and vice versa. I was still fairly young but the more experienced lads had a few problems. Bryan, who had done well as manager of Wigan, always seemed to confront the older players rather than try and work with them. Osman, John O'Neil and Paul Ramsey found it difficult at times and others were affected as well, so it was maybe no surprise things didn't work out that season. We were relegated and that was particularly sore even though I was second-top scorer after Alan Smith. I had signed for Leicester to play in the First Division and it was a major disappointment to know that wasn't going to continue to be the case. But at the same time I felt City were too good to stay out of the top flight so there was never any possibility of me looking elsewhere.

And there were lighter moments during the season. We had signed defender Steve Walsh from Wigan, a real assassin, but he took some stick for an off-the-field incident. We went to Trinidad and Tobago to play a game and Walshy watched the *Karate Kid II* movie on the flight. Afterwards he admitted he was surprised it hadn't been filmed in English because that would have made it far more watchable than it had been in German. Then one of the lads pointed out he hadn't switched stations on the channel selector.

On the same trip Ali Mauchlen decided it would be a good idea to greet some of his teammates coming out of the lift by spraying them with foam from the hotel fire-extinguisher. The only problem there was that it was a type of liquid spray and it nearly blinded the lads. It was also white, so they all emerged looking like Casper the Ghost. These are the kind of daft things players get up to but there's never any harm meant and Leicester was a good club for that kind of mucking about.

But the Filbert Street managerial revolving door was in full swing and Hamilton, who never quite got it right, left and in came David Pleat. He had done well at Luton and Spurs but suffered a lot of bad publicity over a kerb-crawling incident. But he arrived at Filbert Street with a fine managerial pedigree and that was all I was concerned about. He brought Gordon Lee with him, another sound football man, and it has to be said that from the moment they arrived I felt I made real progress as a player. There's no doubt in my mind they made me much better. You can always be taught things and therefore you can always learn, and I was a keen student. I was always asking about players like Hoddle, Chris Waddle and

Brian Stein, whom David had worked with before. And it seemed to me he said the right things. I felt I always got good advice and I was influenced quite a bit by that managerial partnership.

By then I was also beginning to be noticed by Scotland, and that vindicated my move south if nothing else did. I never got a sniff of the international scene when I was at Motherwell and it needed me to move to England to prompt some recognition. My first involvement was in a 'B' game against France at Pittodrie and it was there I had my first – but not my last – close look at one Eric Cantona. Andy Roxburgh and Craig Brown, who have been my only two international managers, were in charge and my teammates included Charlie Nicholas and Frank McAvennie. I actually managed a goal in a 1–1 draw and enjoyed the whole occasion immensely – but then again that's always been the case with me where Scotland is concerned. And when you manage to represent your country there's no doubt your profile gets higher.

Leicester, by that time, were trying to get me on a long-term deal, but my agent, Jon Holmes, who also acted for Gary Lineker, drummed it into me that I shouldn't commit myself for too long with the possibility of Freedom of Contract not too far away.

So it was an interesting stage of my career and David Pleat was doing some good business in the transfer market. He bought lads like Nicky Cross, Billy Davies and Peter Weir, and of the three it was the latter who astonished me most. I was constantly amazed at just how talented Peter was. He had remarkable ability. And that was the kind of player David preferred. He was a real football enthusiast who liked to see the game played the right way. He wouldn't be unhappy if we lost 4–3 just as long as we had contributed to a fine game, and he would certainly prefer that to a 1–0 defeat when we hadn't played worth a monkey's. It was an interesting philosophy and not one that is shared by all that many managers. Many people pointed the finger at Pleat because of that and also because some believed his views on the game to be a bit intricate. But my short answer to that would be to say that anyone with any kind of football brain could understand and appreciate him. Others couldn't.

Eventually, however, I began to get a bit restless at Filbert Street. Maybe it was the increasing press speculation about me that did it – it can be difficult when it seems as though just about every club in the world is being linked to a deal for you. That was the case with me and I know for a fact that at one stage no fewer than *twenty-seven* clubs had been suggested by the media as being keen to sign me. Liverpool, Celtic, Seville . . . you name it, the club was there.

I think by then I also appreciated that Leicester was only ever meant to be a stepping-stone for me, just as the club has been for so many others. Don't get me wrong. I enjoyed my time at Filbert Street and they provided me with a great opportunity. I'll always be grateful for that. They had opened up a whole new world to me. When I left Motherwell I had no real idea of how different the standard was in English football or how much fitter I needed to be to survive. So it was a tremendous move for me at the time and I appreciate what they gave me, just as I believe I gave them something in return.

But my horizons had broadened and, despite City's determined efforts to get me to sign a long-term contract, I was digging my heels in over that. Jon Holmes, my agent, had been advising me on pensions and everything related to my earnings, and he wisely instructed me to ignore all City's efforts to bump up my wages. That may sound a bit strange but he knew that, come 1990, a continental side could come in for me and get me for ten times my salary which would have given them a bargain – according to him! – buy for around £300,000. So he knew it could work in my favour to refuse new, increased terms.

It was all a bit unreal for me and, for that matter, for City, who could see thousands of pounds disappearing over the horizon. They really were *very* keen to bump up my wages. It never really bothered me at the time because Jon was looking after all that side of things but it has crossed my mind since that if I was worth so much more, why had it taken City so long to do something about it?

CHAPTER FOUR

Notts Forest 0, Leeds United 1

Brian Clough. Now there are two words more than capable of starting an argument in an empty room. I can understand that because in all my years in football I don't think I have ever met a man so full of contradictions. He had an 'up' side and a 'down' side as far as I'm concerned, and it was the 'down' side that changed the course of my football career. I simply couldn't take to the man and it's basically for that reason that I am now at Leeds United and not Nottingham Forest. But that's jumping ahead of myself slightly.

When I was beginning to attract some serious attention at Leicester City and so many clubs seemed, at least according to the newspapers, to be keen to sign me, the world appeared to be my oyster. Yet for a long time I was firmly convinced that I might only venture a few miles from Filbert Street – to Forest's City Ground to be exact.

I was a long-time admirer of Brian Clough's teams and that stems purely and simply from the fact that they always appeared to me to try and play football. The game is all about passing and playing – at least as far as I'm concerned it is – and Forest seemed to epitomise that. And it's not as if they did that without any success; by the time they were expressing a serious interest in obtaining my services, they were well recognised as one of the foremost clubs in the country. They had won most of the honours the game has to offer, and usually in style. I liked that.

Cloughie, unquestionably, had made ordinary players into near world-beaters and had managed to get even more out of already good footballers. He appeared to me, at least from afar, to be my kind of manager.

So when the Nottingham club started to make interested noises to both Leicester City and myself, it seemed a golden opportunity to let my career progress still further. Clough had a £1 million bid for me accepted by a Leicester board of directors still paranoid about losing me for less than half that amount, so the way was cleared for me to talk to Forest as well. My first meeting was with Ron Fenton and Alan Hill – Cloughie's loyal and faithful men – and after a lengthy chat I was quite happy with the way things were shaping. And after a second meeting, I was more or less convinced that was it. To be frank, I was a Nottingham Forest player in everything but name and it seemed nothing could get in the way of a move to the City Ground. Well, nearly nothing.

Maybe I hadn't reckoned on the bold Brian. I eventually met the great man at Sandyacre Post House just off the M1. He was a bit late, which wasn't the best of starts, but that was just a minor irritation. When he did turn up, though, he made it abundantly clear he wasn't happy that I had Jon Holmes with me even though an agent was part and parcel of most deals by then. Brian's problem seemed to be that Jon had 'taken' players like Peter Shilton and Tony Woodcock away from the club – or at least that was how Clough viewed him even though Holmes was only acting in his clients' interests. The Forest manager really did make it absolutely plain that he didn't want my man there and, on top of arriving late, I have to say I wasn't best impressed with his manner.

Cloughie then went on to admit he had only seen me play once. I could have lived with that admission because I'm sure others at Forest had seen more of me. But he went on: 'You can't head the ball, you can't tackle and you can't chase back.' I was getting bad vibes. He did have the good grace to add: 'But you

can control the ball and you can pass to one of your team-mates.'
Talk about being damned with faint praise.

It was all enough to make me wonder if I could actually
work with the man for the next four years – but even then I
might have given it the benefit of the doubt. Then I saw at first
hand one of the mood swings I had heard about. Cloughie's
reputation went before him wherever he was, but because I
didn't know him, I reserved judgment. Maybe that was just as
well, because as we sat chatting a young waiter in the
background was piling some spoons onto a tray. He was
unintentionally clattering about a bit but it was hardly a major
distraction. So that made Clough's next move all the more
astonishing to me. He stopped our talk and had a real go at the
young lad. It made me distinctly embarrassed and it looked,
and sounded, dreadful. There was absolutely no need for the
row. I was disappointed in him for that unwarranted
exhibition.

It was astonishing altogether. A transfer that had been all
but signed and sealed had fallen apart after a player's meeting
with the man who was going to be his new manager. That's
normally the bit that finalises the whole deal!

So when everything was put together – and, remember,
this was a big move for me – I just had a gut feeling it wasn't
quite right. I couldn't make the money the excuse in any way,
shape or form because it was a phenomenal offer. In fact, at one
point, Cloughie told me I was asking for terms not dissimilar to
those enjoyed by big names like Des Walker, Stuart Pearce and
his own son, Nigel. But in almost the same breath he said he
would give me that kind of money.

So there was nothing wrong with that part of the package.
It was the bit about working with Cloughie I didn't really fancy.
I know dozens of other players have thought exactly the
opposite, gone on to great things and wouldn't have a bad word
to say about Brian. But he wasn't for me and I told Forest so the
next day.

Whatever else you might say about Cloughie, though, he was persistent and he pushed for another meeting. We met again in Leicester when he came over with his reserve side for a game at Filbert Street and once again I saw the Jekyll and Hyde character of the man. This time he was as nice as ninepence. He was the perfect gentleman and could have charmed the birds off the trees. Forest were heading for Tenerife for a break the following day and he insisted both I and my girlfriend, Denise – now my wife – go along with them. But still I had nagging doubts about the whole thing and, in the end, I pulled the plug on it finally by saying no once more.

It's impossible to know what might have happened if I had gone to the City Ground but at the time and now I have no regrets about not signing that deal.

I may not have been too disappointed at the breakdown of that transfer – but I don't think the same could be said for Leicester! They were definitely twitchy about getting their dough but, believe it or not, the cash was not my primary concern. Money is important, I realise that, but the club has to be right for me. I have to feel good about it and be happy going to my work. And I always believe that if you're successful in football you'll be well rewarded anyway, so you're not missing out.

But there's no two ways about the fact that the Forest offer was a hugely attractive one from a financial point of view. So much so, that it scuppered another couple of possible deals. Arsenal showed an interest in me, but as soon as they heard the Forest terms they backed off in a hurry. Celtic, too, made an approach through Tommy Craig who asked me if I would consider talking to the Parkhead club, but I didn't for a second believe they could match Forest's offer so nothing more happened there at that point. In fact, it didn't bother me to go on playing till the summer when I knew a tribunal would have to determine my price tag. The actual fee, after all, wasn't my problem.

I gained my first Scotland cap that April against East Germany, which didn't do my bargaining powers any harm, and then things started to stir on the old transfer front once more. I was included in the international reckoning for a game against Poland the following month and, indeed, for the World Cup that was to follow in Italy. That kind of thing always adds to your credibility and I was delighted. So when the transfer merry-go-round hotted up I was in a position of some strength. I'd had a good season at Filbert Street and I was part of the Scotland squad.

Leeds United were next to express a serious interest but Celtic had stepped in to the frame more seriously as well. I was due to meet Elland Road boss Howard Wilkinson and then Parkhead manager Billy McNeill before I joined the rest of the international squad for the game against the Poles. So I went to Howard's house in Sheffield where the manager and coach Mick Hennigan outlined the details of their interest. The pair of them talked a good game and I left well impressed by their desire and commitment, if not their financial package.

I know I've just said that money wasn't my god, and neither it was. But remember too that I admitted it was important and the Leeds deal didn't even get close to matching the offer I'd had from Forest. Ironically, the Nottingham club were still showing some kind of interest, so that helped, but I got good vibes from the Leeds management team − just as I got not-so-good ones from Brian Clough − and that was enough to keep me talking. Howard was so enthusiastic about everything to do with United. There was a buzz about him that suggested he and the club were going to explode onto the scene. They had just won promotion and Wilkinson insisted they were on a roll. I knew, too, from playing against them often enough, that they had a fantastic support home and away and occasionally I had got on the wrong side of those fans because I had scored a few goals against their heroes while playing for Leicester.

It was all beginning to feel quite good and there was

another huge plus about the club that couldn't possibly be ignored. Gordon Strachan, a marvellous player and a smashing guy, had already gone to Elland Road. He had quit Manchester United to take on the new challenge with Leeds, and although I didn't know him very well, I had played against him and had heard a fair bit about him because he had done so well for his clubs and his country throughout a glittering career. When I weighed it all up there was a powerful argument in favour of United.

So next in line was Leeds' managing director, Bill Fotherby, a flamboyant character who is absolutely fanatical about the club. But by then, just to complicate the plot a little, Seville had realised that they could get me for £300,000, and that even with wages on top, they just might be able to do themselves a favour. But that petered out after they signed Austrian Toni Polster and the long-running saga was heading back Elland Road way.

Nothing was straightforward, though, and Howard Wilkinson left for Italy to help Bobby Robson's England prepare for the World Cup. But the last instructions Howard gave before he left Elland Road were to sign me and that task fell to Fotherby. He carried out the task to the letter!

But it took some tough negotiating before the deal all fell into place and, when it did, poor Bill was a bit concerned about the whole package he had offered me. He had a wry smile on his face when he phoned Howard and woke him up in his Italian hotel to tell him that the deal was done. That left me to call Billy McNeill and I got the Celtic boss out of his bed as well. Billy, though, took it very well and wished me all the best, which I appreciated.

So that was it. I was a Leeds United player with the fee to Leicester to be decided by a tribunal, which later settled on a figure of £1 million.

I had only met Howard Wilkinson the once but I had been hugely impressed by him and, for that matter, by Bill Fotherby. The pair of them had me believing we would win the League the first season back upstairs, and I liked that. I liked, too, the fact that Elland Road has always had a good Scottish influence about it. Lads like Gordon McQueen, Billy Bremner, Joe Jordan, Peter Lorimer, Eddie Gray and others had all done well there. They were all part of Don Revie's golden era, but since those days United had been a bit of a sleeping giant. Now, though, it was stirring and I was pleased to be part of it all. I just knew, from my dealings with those fans as well, that it was going to be a good place to play my football.

In the end, I might add, the Leeds package wasn't as good as the one I rejected from Nottingham Forest . . . but it was good enough. I moved from Second Division wages into the top flight salary-wise, and although I was by no means the best-paid player in the country, I was quite satisfied with my lot. That was down to Jon Holmes because, although a player must always, obviously, have the final say in any move, there are a lot of ins and outs he doesn't need to be involved with which he can leave to a trusted agent. If those bits and pieces are handled properly – as they are with me – then it can take a lot of the pressure off. There are, however, agents and agents. Jon, who has represented a lot of sportsmen over the years, has been good for me. He has helped me in many different ways and I would have to advise a talented young player to get himself an agent – the right one – even though some clubs aren't comfortable dealing with them.

The postscript to that long and winding road to Leeds was my announcement, when I joined the Scotland squad for the World Cup, that I was going to Italy as a Leeds United player. It had a certain ring to it and I was delighted the transfer saga was resolved. I could have gone to that 1990 World Cup as a free agent, and if I had starred for Scotland it might all have added another zero to my wages. But maybe it's just as well it was sorted out before I went because I never got a kick of the ball in Italy!

CHAPTER FIVE

First Season at Elland Road

Just when you think you've made it in football something comes along to remind you you're really just a novice. Or, as someone once said: 'Just as you bend down to pick up a medal, you get a kick up the backside.'

I was feeling quite pleased with myself after signing for Leeds because, after all, I was a million-pound player, at least according to the tribunal. So when I went on holiday after the World Cup I felt a bit of a star. Denise and I went to Florida and had a great time. We met a couple from London with whom we became very friendly and, in the general chat, they got to know I was a footballer.

The World Cup finals were still going at the time – Scotland, as ever, had been knocked out at the first stage – and when it came to the semis I was keen to watch on the telly along with this lad from London. He actually wasn't that interested in the game – and the reason I'm making that point will become clear. Much later, after they had gone home, he mentioned to friends that he had met this footballer on holiday called Gary *Pallister*. It was only when someone pointed out to him that the Manchester United star had still been in Italy with England at that time that he realised it had been me he was with! So much for fame. Despite that, we're still good pals.

At least it brought me back down to earth with a vengeance, and any other notions of stardom were finally dismissed when I turned up at Elland Road for pre-season training. Howard Wilkinson had also bought Chris Whyte and John Lukic to strengthen the squad for the first season back up, and I think the early days were a shock to us all. I returned feeling pretty fit after being in training with the Scots lads in Italy, and I had also kept myself in reasonable nick on my holidays. Or so I thought.

I was kidding myself, obviously. On the first few runs under Wilkinson's watchful eye even the goalkeepers were beating me. I was fighting fit all right – fighting for breath and fit for the bucket. I was well off the pace in those runs and the only consolation – minor though it was – was that Whyte was back there alongside me. I thought I had signed for Leeds Harriers or a local athletics team of some sort.

I had a lot of catching up to do to get to the same level of fitness as the lads who had been through a Wilkinson pre-season before, but at least it let me know quickly – very quickly – what I had to do. It was a bit of a shock to my system. But that also applied to just about everything to do with the club.

There was a tremendous sense of optimism about United and, indeed, about the city, where everyone seemed to want to wish me well and it was clear the fans shared the club's ambitions. They all wanted Leeds to get back to where they had been previously under Don Revie, when United were challenging for all the honours all the time. So did we, of course, but the expectations were so enormous it was a bit frightening.

Still, when you looked around the squad there was no apparent reason why that shouldn't be the case. It didn't take me long to realise, for instance, the enormous respect everyone had for Gordon Strachan and just what a massive influence he was on everything. But Gordon wasn't the only quality player at Elland Road and I quickly found others to admire. In my own middle-of-the-park area I teamed up with Strach, David Batty and Gary Speed, which I still believe to be one of the most formidable midfields there has been anywhere for quite some time: Strach had marvellous all-round ability, I could pass the ball a bit, Batts had the necessary bite and Speedo lived up to his name with his pace. It was very well balanced and it promised much as soon as I had the chance to survey the lads around me.

There was no reason to change my opinion after the first game on our return to the First Division. We were away to Everton – and I can think of easier places to go than Goodison in the circumstances. But it all went brilliantly from the moment I went out onto the pitch beforehand and saw for myself the incredible backing the supporters give Leeds United. There must have been 15,000 of our fans inside the stadium well before kick-off and I knew for certain then, as if I didn't know before, that I had made the right move a couple of months earlier. The three new lads in the United squad – Lukic, Whyte and myself – got a special cheer and, although I know it sounds corny, we went out again feeling ten foot tall.

And we murdered Everton. We went 2–0 ahead before half-time and eventually won 3–2 courtesy of goals from Chris Fairclough, Speed and Imre Varadi, while Pat Nevin and John Ebbrell got their strikes. It was a tremendous victory – away from home – to kick-start the new season. Ironically, though, it was overshadowed by a bizarre incident. During the interval, with his side two goals down, Everton keeper Neville Southall elected to sit with his back against his goalpost and didn't go back to the dressing-room at all. He was having a few problems with the club at the time and he was later fined a week's wages for his sit-in. But that protest – or whatever it was – definitely diverted attention away from our win.

Yet the Leeds lads knew how important it had been to get off to a good start and we were well pleased with ourselves. We knew if we could pick up good results like that on our travels then we wouldn't be too far away from the top at the end of the day because we always fancied ourselves at Elland Road.

And why not? The Leeds ground is a fortress and, to be honest, we feel invincible in front of our own fans. It's a cauldron for visiting teams and I think if you asked any other player where they least fancy visiting, Elland Road would be right up there. It's heaven for us most of the time but hell for the opposition.

I say *most* of the time because although the fans give us enormous backing they're not above a bit of barracking of their own players if they feel they deserve it. I can't imagine any Leeds player has escaped a bit of flak at one time or another. I know I've had it and it's not pleasant, but if you're strong you get on with your game and get over it and soon you're back in their good books. If you're weak, well, maybe you go under.

But in the early weeks of that first season back the supporters didn't have too much to moan about. We were steady if not spectacular and the worst results we had in the opening couple of months were a defeat at Luton closely followed by another against Tottenham and then, in October, we lost to Queens Park Rangers.

But we had some good moments as well and we beat Nottingham Forest 3–1 with yours truly getting on the scoresheet – and enjoying a sweet moment. And big Lee Chapman – more of him later – was scoring like it was going out of fashion. So we were never too far away from the top-of-the-table action and I was well settled.

We had a fairly grim start to 1991 when we lost away at Liverpool and Norwich in quick succession and, in fact, it was a dodgy spell all round because we crashed to Southampton, Arsenal and Crystal Palace as well before we got our act together again.

By then the chances of improving on our position of fourth weren't that bright but we did have a couple of amazing matches between then and the end of the season. In April, for example, we lost 4–5 to Liverpool in an astonishing Elland Road fixture. We pulled back from four goals down thanks in no small way to a Chappy hat-trick and the big man even had one disallowed for a foul on Mike Hooper. But his efforts weren't quite enough in that remarkable game and it was the same story on the last day of the League season when he scored twice but we still managed to lose 4–3 to, of all teams, Forest.

So we finished fourth top behind Arsenal, Liverpool and Palace and, in the overall scheme of things, it wasn't a bad way to return to the First Division.

And we had a good run in the Rumbelows Cup when we saw off, among others, my old club Leicester and Aston Villa before we lost 3–1 on aggregate to Manchester United in the semi-final.

In the FA Cup we had an epic tie against Arsenal that was longer-running than *Coronation Street*. We drew 0–0 at Highbury, then 1–1 at Elland Road after extra time. Back to London for a second replay and we stayed level after another 0–0 draw which meant a fourth game – and this time the Gunners beat us 2–1. That tournament has never done me many favours and I don't think I ever played in a winning team for Leicester in the competition!

But, as ever with professional players, it is the League Championship that is the one that sums up your season. And we all knew we had shown enough at times to suggest we could do even better next year. But we didn't know then just how much better.

CHAPTER SIX

How the League was Won

There are three vastly different ways of looking at Leeds United's fantastic Premiership Championship success of season 1991–92.

One is to believe that, rather than us winning the title, Manchester United lost it. The second is to consider that the arrival of Eric Cantona somehow swung the whole thing our way and that the Frenchman won the League on his own. And the third is to look objectively at a tremendous effort from everyone at Elland Road and to accept that the club deserved the triumph.

It won't come as a major surprise to know that I happen to believe in the third option. And I'm tired of people being unable – or unwilling – to see past the first two. Manchester United's self-destruction and Cantona's signing were unquestionably contributing factors to the Leeds success, but they weren't the main ones. Instead, let me give you another few reasons:

- Manager Howard Wilkinson bought wisely and well before a ball was kicked.

- We had outstanding individual performances all through the team, all through the season.

- We played exceptionally well as a unit and lost only four

League matches all season.

• We had a great team spirit.

They were among the real reasons for our glory run and maybe at times they have been disregarded as people have looked elsewhere for the basis of our success. But it's worth examining in more depth the season in general because it was, for whatever reasons, a memorable one.

The manager, mindful of the need to improve the squad after the previous season, splashed the cash – £4 million of it – to capture left-back Tony Dorigo from Chelsea, Rod and Ray Wallace from Southampton and Steve Hodge from Nottingham Forest. With the exception of young Ray, they all played a significant part. Howard is always keen to add players to the squad whenever possible, a plan perhaps adopted from Liverpool during their great years when they bought from a position of strength rather than through desperation. So he got through big money, confident it was well spent.

The side – Dorigo and Rod Wallace apart, because Hodge spent a lot of time on the substitutes' bench – was otherwise more or less the same as the one that had finished fourth the previous year. That meant John Lukic in goal with Mel Sterland, Chris Whyte and Chris Fairclough a formidable barrier ahead of him, then the midfield quartet of me, Strach, Batts and Speedo, with Chappy up front. Others, of course, played their part, and guys like John McClelland, Carl Shutt, Jon Newsome and Eric Cantona all made big contributions.

As ever, a good start was vital and we got off to a flyer when I scored the only goal of the game at home to Nottingham Forest. We were particularly pleased to get that victory under our belts because our season had already been hampered and started late because of rebuilding work at Crystal Palace's Selhurst Park. The ground was unavailable for the opening day so we were three points behind Manchester United, for instance, even before we started! But we built well on that opening game and continued to get some useful results.

There were a few dramas in the opening couple of months. I remember a 1–1 draw with United at Old Trafford when I thought I was dying. It must have been a hundred degrees in the Old T bowl and the players were gasping for breath all the time. We were gasping again at the beginning of September – in surprise – when Batts scored his first goal for nearly four years in the 3–0 victory over Manchester City! And there was a win over Liverpool during the same spell which was Leeds' first over the Anfield side for eighteen years.

So all was well until we came up against Palace in the match that should have started the season but instead was postponed until October. A late, late goal from Mark Bright did the damage to Leeds and a late, late Geoff Thomas tackle did the damage to me. I had to retire from the proceedings after that challenge and then again in the next game against Sheffield United when my ankle was still causing me pain.

Fortunately, the Palace result was only a hiccup for the team but it certainly caused me some trouble. Because I was still feeling the ankle knock a bit I was put on the bench for the next game against Notts County and I don't mind admitting I had a petted lip at the prospect. I felt that if I had been fit enough for the Sheffield game then I was fit enough to face County. So I felt I had a bit of a point to prove when I went on – and I promptly scored from around thirty-five yards to make that point. I thought that would show the manager that I shouldn't have been left out in the first place. But even I have to admit the argument was diluted somewhat when substitute McAllister was in turn substituted! And that ankle problem stayed with me on and off all through the season, although at least I didn't miss any more matches.

A 1–0 win over Oldham at the end of October was remarkable only because Manchester United lost at Sheffield Wednesday the same day – and that meant we were at the top of the table for the first time since 1974. And we stayed there for a while as we continued another terrific unbeaten run. We were live on the box as we trounced Aston Villa and began to believe television coverage was a good omen because we turned in another scintillating performance for the cameras in mid-January when we hammered Sheffield Wednesday 6–1.

While these victories undoubtedly made the rest of the country really sit up and take notice, they were also significant for other reasons. The brilliant performance at Villa Park came after an astonishing tactical switch by Howard Wilkinson. The manager played big John McClelland in that match after he had been out for a while, and he played him specifically to watch Villa's flying winger, Tony Daley. Big John, an outstanding player, was basically doing his own training at Elland Road by then because he was, after all, getting on a bit, and it seemed a strange decision to put him on one of the fastest players in the game. But Mac was magnificent in a tremendous 4–1 win.

Howard made a few of those little changes throughout the season and although they weren't particularly noticed, they undoubtedly contributed to our success. And in the high-scoring game against Wednesday, the manager had to contend without Strach and Batts, who were both out injured. David had had a wound in his foot stitched up wrongly, but in the end it was the rest of the lads who were in stitches as we murdered the Hillsborough side. It could even have been more than six but the manager and Mel Sterland, who are Sheffield people, seemed quite happy.

There was nothing particularly remarkable for a couple of weeks after that – until we came up against Oldham at Boundary Park, a ground that has always given us problems. It's a terrible place for Leeds and on this occasion it was wall-to-wall mud. We had signed Eric Cantona on a contract till the end of the season but heaven only knows what he thought about English football after his first look! Or, for that matter, what he thought about Leeds United because even though he came off the substitutes' bench – not quite what he was used to in the first place – we lost our second match of the season 2–0.

It was February by then so it was fairly well into the season before the Frenchman even joined us. But to be fair to Eric, he settled quickly and scored his first goal against Luton at the end of that month.

Perhaps the strangest thing about that season was the fact that the four games we lost were all to sides we might have been expected to beat in the circumstances. Palace and Oldham had done us and Queens Park Rangers trounced us 4–1, with Chris Whyte being sent off to complete a miserable ninety minutes. And at the beginning of April we lost another four goals – to Manchester City – to install their city rivals, United, firmly in the driving seat for the title.

Howard Wilkinson, I must say, remained very calm even after that horror show and he continued to use Cantona quite cleverly. He played the French star a few times after an initial period on the bench and then put him back among the substitutes again where he knew he was an important weapon for us. If things weren't going well and the fans began to murmur then Eric was there to lift them – and us – again. But because he was used so sparingly you could hardly say he won us the League. He was an influence, certainly, but if you're looking to who won the title for Leeds United, you need to look in other directions. There was a nucleus of players – around fourteen of us – who played in the majority of games. But at that stage of the season those players still had a lot of work to do. There were five games remaining – 450 minutes of football – to decide the outcome.

We were very definitely second favourites but in the Elland Road dressing-room there was a quiet confidence that we could still achieve the seemingly impossible. We had heard a few rumblings from Old Trafford and the fact that they looked under all sorts of pressure indicated that maybe all wasn't well in Manchester. So there was a genuine feeling that if we kept up the pressure, the wheels might come off their bogie. And, when we looked at the run-in, that view was confirmed. We had still to play Chelsea, Coventry and Norwich at home and Liverpool and Sheffield United away. United had Luton, West Ham and Liverpool away and Forest and Spurs at Old Trafford. Those fixtures, we felt, gave us the edge. But it was all to play for and if United had kept their heads and we hadn't kept the pressure on then I suppose they would have won it. But they didn't and we did.

We beat Chelsea comfortably and then drew at Anfield while they drew against Luton and lost at home to Forest. That all made the next game for both teams absolutely vital.

I notched a penalty in our 2–0 victory over Coventry and United, incredibly, then lost a couple of days later at Upton Park. Batts, Speedo and I were at a karaoke evening as part of Jim Beglin's testimonial as the news came in that United had lost 1–0 and I can't imagine our singing has ever sounded sweeter!

That set it up nicely for the finale to the season with just a couple of games left for both teams. But we knew that we could beat Sheffield United first and foremost and, importantly, we also realised that Manchester United would get absolutely no favours from Liverpool. The Anfield and Old Trafford rivalry is probably even more intense than it is between the Leeds fans and the United supporters, so it was always going to be a difficult one for Alex Ferguson's team. They weren't happy, either, that their Merseyside meeting was to take place a couple of hours after our visit to Bramall Lane. That meant, with a win being enough to give us the title, that they had no real chance of getting back at us if we did secure the three points.

And, somehow, we did just that, and in an extraordinary match. Bramall Lane seems to me always to have a whirlwind of rubbish floating around the pitch, which is never a great start. And neither was a 28th-minute goal from Blades striker Alan Cork. But a scrambled Rod Wallace effort gave us an equaliser and Jon Newsome put us into the lead – only for big Lee

Chapman to score an own goal. It was all Mickey Mouse stuff, really. And the comic cuts continued when Blades defender Brian Gayle headed over his own keeper to give us a 3–2 victory. There were mutterings after that game about bungs and dodgy deals but Gayle was simply unlucky – and we were the beneficiaries.

And how we celebrated. The dressing-room was pandemonium and it was a fantastic feeling to realise we were the best team in the country. That is what the title proves and any bleating to the contrary is just that. We have had to swallow our disappointment at times when maybe we've felt we deserved better but at the end of the day no one has ever argued against the fact that the side that finishes top of the heap deserves to.

Our triumph was all the more incredible because no one in the squad had been there before. Wee Strach had certainly done it with Aberdeen, but this was different, so it's maybe no surprise that we all let our hair down in style. Batts, Eric Cantona and I ended back in Lee Chapman's living-room doing an ITV interview and the four of us sat looking quite calm holding what appeared to be mugs of tea. The difference was that the rather inelegant mugs held nothing but champagne and more champagne. And gradually I think it must have shown! Television did a link-up with Manchester United manager Alex Ferguson and he was clearly on a major downer while we were jumping about demented. It was bedlam. Then the telly guy asked Chappy, who must have insisted he spoke French, to interpret for Eric Cantona. The question was asked via big Lee who, in his best *'Allo 'Allo* accent, then passed it on to Eric. It was bizarre and even Batts was moved to suggest he could have done the French bit just as well.

But it was all good fun and it continued from there to the Flying Pizza restaurant in town where the owner is a United fanatic. When the players and their wives walked in we all got a standing ovation and it was really a free-for-all for the rest of the night. After that there seemed to be a never-ending list of functions to be attended that week and everyone enjoyed going along to as many as we could even though there was a final League game to be played, against Norwich City. That was always going to be a bit of an anti-climax and I'm sure the last thing the Norwich lads wanted was to be part of our celebrations. They probably simply wanted to get the game over and done with and get back down the road.

There was a party atmosphere inside a packed Elland Road when we were presented with the Championship trophy, and it was a sweet moment. Rod Wallace somehow managed to get the only goal of the game and then the afternoon was spoiled a little – but not too much – by some of our fans getting on to the pitch. They were desperate for some sort of souvenir of the occasion, and I lost my boots and shin pads. But it could have been worse. I could have been Speedo. He got an accidental – well, we think it was accidental – right hook. Mind you, after the week he'd had, I doubt if he felt it anyway, and in reality nothing could spoil the moment for the lads. There had been a few ups and downs getting to the end result, but over the piece I don't think anyone in the squad was found wanting.

Howard, of course, did brilliantly and there were times – like when he put McClelland on Daley – that he engineered a clever change in our style. He also asked Batts to keep a close eye on Everton's Peter Beardsley in one game and to do that David had to forsake his own style a bit. Chris Fairclough was another who changed his ways occasionally. These were all relatively minor tactical switches but they were important to our success.

Individually, there were a load of outstanding performances through the season but if I had to pick out a couple of players – and I don't particularly like to – they would have to be Strach and Chappy. Gordon was immense and, as skipper, led by example throughout the term. He really did play a captain's part. And Lee had a fabulous season. He spent a few weeks on the sidelines with a broken wrist but still managed sixteen vital goals in the League. But it really was a team effort, as these things always have to be. There is never any room for passengers in a title-winning squad.

But even after that final game against Norwich, when somehow the lads shrugged off a week of celebrations to get another result, the partying wasn't over. We had a black-tie dinner at Elland Road after that match when we all looked the part except Eric who, being Eric, turned up in a loud Versace shirt. He genuinely wasn't trying to stand out from the crowd. It was simply his way and no one minded. But what I was concerned about was the awful moment when I thought I had lost my medal. My heart sank and I grew more and more frantic before we found it in Denise's handbag.

And after all that, there was still the open-top bus ride to a civic reception in Leeds city centre. That was quite unforgettable. We left Elland Road and the lads thought there might be a few hundred fans at the square when we arrived, but as soon as we headed through Beeston and Holbeck we couldn't believe our eyes. *Thousands* of supporters lined the streets all the way and unofficial estimates for the number who turned up in the centre itself range from 200,000 to quarter of a million. It would be easy to dismiss the significance of all that but it was very emotional for the squad to know just what their achievements had meant to so many people.

And when we reached the end of that remarkable journey, we all addressed the fans individually simply to say thank you for their support through the season. All the lads did the honours and had a few words, basically just applauding the fans. Then Eric took the microphone and declared: 'I don't know why I love you but I do.' He had the place in uproar and it was a fantastic sight.

Inevitably when all the dust settled there were comparisons between our squad and the one coached and managed so brilliantly by Don Revie in an earlier Leeds era. Howard, indeed, had been criticised long before for getting rid of the team pictures and reminders from around Elland Road of that great Billy Bremner side. It was a bit unfair because the manager had enormous respect for that previous team but he just didn't want us to have to cope with their success being rubbed in constantly. But we knew, even after our title success, that we had a long way to go before we could even be mentioned in the same breath as that great squad.

I have absolutely no problem dealing with that team and, in fact, I went out of my way to buy the videos of their exploits because they were a *great* side. They were also a bit unlucky because there's no doubt in my mind that they could have won far more than they did. And when I talk to lads like Eddie Gray, Norman Hunter, Billy, Johnny Giles and others, they admit that themselves. And these guys are all still around Elland Road quite a lot. They are keen to see the current side do well, just as we admire their efforts.

The challenge for this squad, though, is to match or better those efforts. Guys like Bremner and Giles were masters of their craft with their passing and their vision and, indeed, their understanding. I personally would love to take bits of their game and make myself a better player because, as I've said elsewhere, you never stop learning in this profession.

But, overall, that title year was a glorious one for everyone who has ever been connected with Leeds. It was also a rewarding one financially for the players but we simply accepted whatever the club gave us and there was no hard bargaining about Championship bonuses. Money isn't forever but that medal is, and when he's old enough to appreciate what it's all about, I'll take great delight in giving it to my son Jake.

CHAPTER SEVEN

The King and I

Eric Cantona is a magnificent footballer and as brilliant a player as I have played with or against throughout my career. Yet, like so many others who are touched by greatness, there is a less attractive element there or thereabouts, lurking just under the surface. It is an indefinable thing, but it surfaces so often that it tends to detract from the other aspects of the man. And he is a person I happen to like. I got to know Eric fairly well when he was with Leeds. We enjoyed a few nights out together and he was good company. But there is a bit of him that I and a lot of others will never understand. Again, isn't that generally the way with a genius?

Eric has proved a complex and perplexing person ever since he arrived in England for a 'trial' with Sheffield Wednesday. That in itself was a bit strange. I've never quite been able to work out why the Hillsborough boss, Trevor Francis, felt he had to watch Eric in training before he signed him. It's amazing that Trevor, who spent a fair bit of time abroad himself during his career, should have deemed it necessary to watch a proven French international play on grass. Remember, when Eric arrived in England, it was mid-winter and he only had a chance to show the Wednesday boss his talents on astroturf.

Howard Wilkinson had no such reservations, and when Wednesday failed to follow through their initial interest, the Leeds manager did it for them. It was an audacious swoop, and to get a player of that undoubted skill and ability for around a million pounds was a steal, really. But then Howard always could recognise talent!

It was a very interesting signing. Some of the lads who watched football all the time, either live or on television, knew a fair bit about Eric anyway. And Gordon Strachan had actually played against him for Scotland. The wee man later loved to recall a famous, but slightly unfortunate, quote from a well-known international manager (who, to save his own embarrassment, shall remain nameless) who declared: 'Cantona is a poor man's Joe Jordan.'

That's not how Strach recalled his first close-up look at the brilliant Frenchman. He had seen Eric give Scotland defender Richard Gough a very hard time in that match and he knew we were getting a good player.

And when Eric arrived at Elland Road there was an early sign of just how good he was. He spoke what is basically a football language and gelled immediately with the rest of the lads, which was a good sign from the start. He added spice to the squad and Lee Chapman, who at various times had led the front line on his own, supported occasionally by the likes of Carl Shutt, Imre Varadi and Rod Wallace, was particularly pleased to see him.

But the manager astonished many people by not using Eric that much. In fact, by the end of our title-winning season, he had only started six games and been substitute in another nine, though he had weighed in with three goals. He also became an instant hit with the Elland Road fans and there is no doubt he made things happen. He scored goals and he made them for others with just one touch or one spectacular piece of vision. His second goal for the club was a marvellous one. It was against Wimbledon and it came after a surging sixty-yard run. His last of that brief season for him was another classic – a brilliant solo effort against Chelsea.

I think he found it a bit difficult and frustrating being on the bench so often, but he contributed to our Championship win in some style even though, as I've said before, he didn't win the title on his own. I saw enough of his touches in that short spell to realise what exceptional quality he had. Yet there were times when Eric did something extra special again and was able to leave us all gasping in disbelief. It happened once in a pre-season outing in Ireland. We were playing Shelbourne and although it's a little difficult to put into words what he did – and to do it justice – I'll try.

The ball came across to him and he cushioned it immediately. He then touched it away to his right with backspin on it but he turned left and then, as the poor defender paid to get back in with his pie and Bovril, Eric was off and running. David Batty and I just looked at each other and shook our heads. It was possibly the most remarkable piece of individual skill I've ever witnessed.

Away from the pitch he was never any problem at the time. He was a great guy any time we went out, and he was easily pleased with everything we did. I think that showed even in the houses he bought when he first came to Leeds and then moved on. He had simple tastes and wasn't at all materialistic.

His next season at the club was a big one for everyone, with the prospect of defending our title being augmented by the possibility of glory in the European Cup. It was exciting, and Eric blitzed into the new season with a hat-trick against Liverpool as Leeds won the Charity Shield in a seven-goal thriller.

But there wasn't too much in the way of glory for Eric or Leeds after that. We struggled as a team to match the consistency of the previous year from the start. The first part of the season, to be fair, wasn't too bad and Eric actually scored fairly freely – another hat-trick against Spurs and a double against Oldham – as we stumbled into the defence of the Championship.

But it was in Europe that things went drastically wrong first and foremost. Our European Cup saga is covered in more detail elsewhere in this book but since I'm talking here of Eric I have to say he was a big disappointment for us in the first game we had in the competition in Stuttgart. The Germans eventually beat us 3–0 and Eric, when so much was expected of him, was nowhere to be seen. In fact, he was eventually replaced by Carl Shutt over there.

Yet the absolute opposite can be said of his performance back at Elland Road in the second leg a fortnight later. He was quite brilliant that night as we won 4–1 and, indeed, he scored a vital goal. The tie, though, had still to be decided because the Germans fielded an ineligible player and it took a third game in Barcelona to sort it all out. And once more, in the magnificent Nou Camp Stadium, Eric didn't cover himself in glory.

But we got through, which was really the main thing, and that lined up the famous 'Battle of Britain' against Rangers. It was a fantastic experience to play in those two games but Eric, as he had been twice against Stuttgart, was substituted at Ibrox. If he had given Richard Gough a hard time in an international then the Scotland star got his own back over those two matches. Eric managed a goal as we crashed out of the tournament at Elland Road but otherwise he hardly had a kick against Gough. I think everyone, probably even Eric himself, had expected more. So that was a disappointment and maybe the writing was on the wall from then on.

He was put back on the substitutes' bench again around the time of those Euro ties and that probably didn't help either. He clearly became a bit unhappy and the first place to recognise that in any player at any time is the dressing-room. I think the players realised the love affair between player and club was cooling. There was no dramatic fall-out as far as I'm aware but the players are quick to sense when something wasn't quite right, and that was the case with Eric.

But what no one – and I mean no one – expected was where his inevitable transfer took him. The news that he was going to Manchester United sent shockwaves through Elland

Road and further afield. I don't think the lads could quite believe he was going to Old Trafford but we are all professionals and, although there was a sense of disbelief initially, we quickly got over it.

Not so everyone else, though. There was outrage in the city where no one could understand how Howard Wilkinson and the club had dared sell Cantona to our hated rivals. The fans went at it a bit and the manager came in for some fairly fierce criticism. But there are two things to be pointed out. The first is that I believe United wanted their money back and got it and more from Manchester United. And the second is that the supporters should trust the manager to make a decision he feels is in the best interests of the club. In this instance, Howard clearly didn't want Eric's unhappiness spreading through the dressing-room.

I could understand that because it wasn't the best of times anyway. We weren't going well in the League and that Euro defeat left us all as flat as a pancake. Basically, we were in trouble and in those circumstances we needed players to kick, bite and scratch to help us through a difficult season. Everyone knows that's not Eric's game. So when he moved on there was no bitterness among the players and to a man we all realised he would go on and do well at Old Trafford. And that, of course, is how it proved.

I would say, however, the Leeds players have been a bit upset by some of the remarks Eric is alleged to have made since he left Elland Road. I'm personally surprised that he has declared he was never given the ball to his feet when he was with us. That, really, is an insult. The Leeds players worked hard for Eric and grafted to adjust so the team could get the best out of him. It is irritating to say the least to hear that 'only Manchester United play the game the way it should be played' and that all his spell at Elland Road did was get him used to the English style in general. Gordon Strachan and Gary Speed aren't exactly kick-and-rush players and although we had strong defenders as every team in the country has, including Manchester United, I believe we had other good players as well.

But Eric, on and off the pitch, is different and you have to live with that. His biggest problem is undoubtedly his temperament. We never saw too much of the dark side of that when he was with us, but it has reared up time and time again since he left. I think it must go with the territory of being something of a genius, even if that in no way excuses some of his excesses. He is never too far away from a drama and he is constantly on a short fuse. Playing where he does puts him in pole position to be kicked and goaded and baited, but Gary Lineker managed to get through a tremendous career without a booking, far less anything else, so it can clearly be done. But not by Eric.

And I simply can't condone some of his actions even though, as I say, I like him. There is no excuse, however much stick you get, to do what he did and react the way he did at Crystal Palace last season. Every player playing away from home usually gets some abuse but you simply have to turn the other cheek and get on with it. And some of his on-the-field challenges have been dreadful. There are no two ways about that.

But if I can't defend his actions, I also can't believe they are pre-planned. It is spur-of-the-moment madness and he bitterly regrets it as soon as the incident is over. I should know – I've been on the receiving end of one of his more enthusiastic challenges. He came in at me with two feet – late – though fortunately I saw it coming and managed to avoid the worst of it. He still caught me a bit, though, and the incident was highlighted over and over again on television. Maybe it could all have been even worse. But I picked myself up quickly and also helped Eric to his feet which possibly diluted the affair a bit. I suppose I could have got Eric sent off but I can't accept that kind of reaction has any part in our game and it's certainly not my instinct to lie down and roll about. Don't get me wrong. I'm not

Mother Teresa but there's no way I would deliberately get a fellow professional sent off. Eric, it seems, can do that for himself.

It's a shame because he really is such a great, great player. He's a big lad but has a wonderful touch and does some unbelievable things which just seem to come naturally to him. It would be great if it was just those remarkable skills – and nothing else – that we could watch and envy.

CHAPTER EIGHT

The Captain's Crew

Gordon Strachan, Vinny Jones, Chris Whyte, Alan Smith, Paul Ramsey, Ali Mauchlen, Lee Chapman, Tony Yeboah . . . there are a few contrasting personalities and players in that lot. I've had the pleasure and privilege of playing alongside them, and others, at Motherwell, Leicester City and Leeds United. And Strach simply must top the list.

He has influenced me a lot through my career and he is the one player in the world I have learned most from. Some of the credit for whatever I have achieved in the game must be down to him because he has been instrumental in helping, encouraging and improving me as I've gone along. And it's really no wonder I have listened to the wee man. He has achieved just about all there is to achieve in football. He's won titles in England and Scotland, he's been Footballer of the Year both sides of the border, he's in Scotland's Hall of Fame for internationalists and he's played for the World XI twice. That's just a few of his successes.

I'm not sure people realise or appreciate just what a marvellous career he has had and what a remarkable player he is. But I certainly do and if former Celtic star Jimmy Johnstone is his great hero then I might as well embarrass the wee man and admit he's one of mine. He was a perfect example to me and he's the same for any youngster. It was great to be able to play in the same midfield as him and I could see better than most just what he was about.

He has a habit, of course, of tormenting opponents and opposition fans alike. When he was at Dundee and then at Aberdeen he was the one player the Celtic fans, for instance, loved to hate more than anyone, and he relished it. He's always had that kind of effect on people. But to have that kind of effect means he must be doing something right and in Gordon's case it was usually more than just one thing. He went on to have a terrific time at Manchester United, where he was an idol for the Old Trafford fans. And then he landed at Elland Road. He has been described as 'the best value for money signing I've ever made' by Howard Wilkinson, and it would be difficult to argue with that. He led United out of the Second Division after his move from Manchester and he gained the respect of any doubting Leeds fans and players then. He went on to skipper the side to the Championship and was a hugely inspirational figure on the way to that title.

I think when Leeds snatched him from Old Trafford it was a signal that the club was going big-time again. They invested heavily in the wee man but the very fact that Leeds was good enough for him attracted others — including me — to the club. And when I saw him leading the pack in those Wilkinson-inspired training runs we used to have, you realised just how fit he was. Howard's routines were good for him but Strach has always looked after himself well, and although he has taken some stick for his porridge-and-banana diets, I have to say they don't look as if they've done him any harm. They have, he insists, prolonged his career, so they can't be all bad.

It has been an education watching him through the years. The way he trains is tremendous because he has such pride in his work. He has always maintained that you can't cruise through training from Monday to Friday and then step up a gear on match days, so Strach has trained the way he has played. And woe betide you if you made a sloppy mistake in training because he then believed you might do the same again when it really

1976

Two cheeky wee monkeys . . . and, no, I don't mean my young brother Craig and I

I love all sports and this is me putting on the style at golf, football and table-tennis

Telegraphic Address: 'STADIUM' Manchester
Telephone: 061-872 1661/2 (Office)
061-872 7771 (Ticket and Match Enquiries)

MANCHESTER UNITED Football Club Ltd

OLD TRAFFORD, MANCHESTER, M16 ORA

Manager:
D. J. SEXTON.

Secretary:
L. OLIVE.

JB/WR

Date as Postmark.

Dear *Thomas McAllister*,

MID-SUMMER SENIOR COURSE, 1979.
Travelling to us:- Monday, 30th July.
Returning:- Friday, 3rd August.

I am aware *Gary* has already had a provisional or verbal
invitation to visit us during the summer holidays.

Dates for the visit are shown above. I hope these prove to be
convenient.

Detailed travel arrangements will be made later but it would help
my administration if you would detach and complete the section below as
an initial step and return to me in the s.a.e. enclosed.

You can be sure we shall take good care of *Gary* whilst with us.
He will at all times be under adult supervision during the day and
evening. We shall try to make the visit rewarding socially and football
wise.

Looking forward to having *Gary* with us.

Regards.

Sincerely,

Joe Brown

J. BROWN,
Chief Scout.

*This is a letter from the club that broke my heart; I loved those trips to Old Trafford and
the bottom fell out of my world when they stopped*

I've carried Ali Mauchlen all through our careers – and here I'm doing it for real!

Left: *There are different ways of celebrating a goal — here's the two-to-tango version with Alan Smith, which I perfected moments after scoring my first goal for Leicester City*
(© Leicester Mercury)

Below: *Rounding Stoke's Peter Fox en route to another goal*
(© Leicester Mercury)

Celebrating with my City teammate, Peter Weir, a tremendous winger
(© Leicester Mercury)

I can't imagine why the Blackburn players on the edge of the area are gearing up for the rebound – I didn't miss this penalty (© Leicester Mercury)

Another successful spot-kick, this time against Dave Beasant (© Leicester Mercury)

Ever since I can remember, it's been my ambition to play for my country – it's such an honour, and I love being involved (© Daily Record)

A goal against Middlesbrough and Brian Laws is just too late (© Leicester Mercury)

Sneaking between Sunderland duo Paul Bracewell (left) and Gary Owers
(© Leicester Mercury)

mattered. It wasn't – or rather isn't – a bad philosophy and it never did him much harm. We have become good friends over the years and play a lot of golf together. He takes that a bit seriously as well! I was sorry when he left Leeds, but it was no surprise when he teamed up again with Ron Atkinson at Coventry and I'm sure he'll be a huge hit there.

Before I had ever even met Strach, though, there was another player who has been quite an influence on me one way or another. Ali Mauchlen and I grew up together in a football sense. We were both at Motherwell and, indeed, joined Leicester City in a joint package. Ali even had a brief spell at Elland Road on loan although he didn't actually play in the first team. He was, as far as I'm concerned, a very underrated player, although part of the reason for that might have been his own recklessness in his early days. He built up a bit of a reputation for himself as an assassin at Kilmarnock and Motherwell but at Fir Park we appreciated him as a player's player. Any scrapping that needed to be done was done by him.

When he and I moved to England, I think it opened his eyes to the different standards he needed to produce, and he improved a lot south of the border. He probably played the best football of his life when David Pleat was manager at Filbert Street because he let Ali play to his strengths, and that in itself is an art for any player.

We had a good partnership for quite a few years and I was pleased when he came to Leeds for his brief spell. He arrived on loan at a time when we needed a little lift and the presence of another player gave everyone a psychological boost. He was on the bench a couple of times as we battled for the title and he enjoyed that although, as ever, he would have much preferred to have been involved.

But all through our long association I have needed eyes in the back of my head. How I survived staying with him is a mystery – although at least his wife Beth and the kids were around to help me. He had what he liked to call the 'Captain's

Barbecue' when we were at Leicester and on one occasion, after a few beers, one of his neighbours was trying particularly hard to impress the City lads who were there enjoying the occasion. Ali, of course, clocked that quicker than most, so he organised a competition to see who could hold his hand over the barbecue longest. The neighbour, naturally, wanted to go first so Ali let him, promptly pushed his hand down on top of the grill and told him he had won!

As a character, Alan Smith was probably the exact opposite of Mauchlen. Yet, as I have mentioned elsewhere, I have never played behind a better striker. I knew about Al's partnership with Gary Lineker even before I arrived at Filbert Street, but when I saw him at first hand I knew he wouldn't be there long: he was too good. In a struggling side he still got goals, and that is no mean feat.

But even when Alan wasn't scoring he was leading the line brilliantly and was weighing in with any number of 'assists'. You don't get 'assists' alongside your name so you don't get much credit for them, but Alan was the master of that. He would be criticised for not scoring by people who didn't see the other work he did. He maybe looks a bit ungainly at times, but he's good with the ball at his feet and he's strong in the air. Ask any midfield man in the country who they like to play behind and they'll mention someone like Smith or Mark Hughes, who always make themselves available. As I say, he's the best all-round striker I have worked with and a thoroughly nice guy into the bargain. If he has a fault it's his Birmingham accent, and when he and fellow Brummie Steve Lynex got together at Filbert Street I was well and truly lost.

Mark Bright at Leicester was another good striker and one of those lads who really helped me settle at Filbert Street. He had the almost impossible task of replacing Lineker but I recall him scoring two goals on his debut when Gary played his first game at Filbert Street for Everton! Unfortunately, he didn't get on with manager Bryan Hamilton, which was a shame because he's a player I would have liked to play with for longer.

Put an Irishman like Paul Ramsey in midfield alongside a fiery Scotsman like Ali Mauchlen, and there's always the chance of fireworks. The two were a bit wary of each other at first at Leicester but they became great friends eventually. Paul was as hard as nails but he could take it as well as give it out. He told me once how he was playing for City against Liverpool and he gave Alan Kennedy a real dull one. I think he was as late as a British Rail train. But five minutes later he was on his way up the tunnel on a stretcher after Graeme Souness had repaid the compliment on his teammate's behalf. Souey was always considerate that way.

Mike Newell was a better striker than some people gave him credit for. He was another who did a lot of unselfish work that maybe wasn't appreciated by anyone other than his teammates.

At Leeds, of course, there have been all sorts of different characters. There was Vinny Jones for a start. I bumped into him first when I was at Leicester – although happily I didn't bump into him literally. He loved giving everyone a touch of the verbals and this was just before the 1990 World Cup when I was hoping to be chosen by Scotland. Vinny's cheerful message, though, went along the lines of: 'You'll never make it to Italy.' What he didn't realise then, and probably hasn't until now, was that wee Strach was right behind him making faces while all I was trying to do was agree with him!

But Vinny was good value nevertheless and he gave Chris Whyte and me a tremendous welcome when we went to Elland Road. We were sitting minding our own business in our hotel one night soon after signing when the phone went and it was Vinny to say he was on his way round to collect us for a night out. He had a driver then and they duly appeared to take us round a few bars. Vinny, honestly, was the king of Leeds at the time after helping the club out of the Second Division. Anyway, he was buzzing and in one of the bars there was a small dance floor and if there's one thing he fancies himself as — apart from a footballer — it's a dancer. We were a bit sceptical but the bold Vinny promptly heard one of his favourite records, did a little tap dance and then went across the floor on his knees John Travolta-style. He was good at it but, there again, he's not a bad player either.

Vinny can play the game and he's made a good career out of it. He's no mug. He has a self-destructive streak that is impossible to defend, but he's now played at international level for Wales and you can't take that away from him. And although his public image has been a bit dented over the years, there is a private side to him that people don't see. He does a tremendous amount of charity work for the handicapped and he is genuinely interested in that. He's by no means all bad and I like him.

David Batty, like Vinny, is a genuine hard man who would front up anyone if he had to. He's a bull of a man and although I always felt he was a very good player for Leeds, he has looked an even better one for Blackburn Rovers. The one disappointment about Batts is his scoring record, but the rest of his game isn't bad compensation. He has just about everything in his locker and is one of the best midfield partners I've had. He's the kind of player you would rather have on your side than against you — and I still have the scar to prove that theory. I once had six stitches in my head after coming off second best in a clash, but I still rate him very highly.

The impact Chris Whyte made at Elland Road can best be demonstrated by the standing ovation he received from the fans when he came to watch us against Tottenham after he had left Leeds for Birmingham. He had had an outstanding season there, just as he had had a terrific spell with us, and the supporters were letting him know they appreciated his efforts. 'Huggy' is a smashing lad and he had a fantastic season when we won the title.

Some people were a bit surprised when Howard Wilkinson splashed out £450,000 to West Bromwich Albion for him but he and Chris Fairclough were a very solid partnership. He was actually the mainstay of the team but was a bit of an unsung hero. He also made a great cup of tea, although I could never understand why he wouldn't do the ironing as well when we roomed together! He actually spent a fair bit of his time on the wrong end of some good-natured stick, and his sartorial elegance was often recognised by the rest of the lads who occasionally hung his gear from the ceiling of the dressing-room.

Gary Speed is another who had an outstanding season when Leeds won the League. But his standards have slipped a bit since then and he admits that himself. He hasn't performed anywhere near as well as he can over the last couple of seasons but I would always want him in my team because he's the kind of lad who will work hard even when he's not playing particularly well. I think he needs to become a bit more selfish and not try to do too much for other people. But there's no doubt in my mind he'll go on and win a lot of caps for Wales. He has learned a lot from players like David Batty and, for that matter, Billy Bremner. He'll get back to his best because he has the right attitude.

What I can't understand, though, is how Gary Speed manages to make a few quid out of modelling. I suppose it's because I pass on all my work to him. He and Gary Kelly – like Ally McCoist at Rangers – are the Leeds pin-ups and they get more fan mail than the rest of the lads put together.

I don't think Lee Chapman has ever necessarily received bags of post from admiring supporters, because he seems to have taken a bit of stick from his own club's fans wherever he's been, and that is grossly unfair. I think Chappy would be the first to admit he's not the most refined of strikers, but his goals record is the best answer he can provide for any critics. His haul is up there with the best. Leeds certainly missed his goals when he left us because first of all they took United into the top flight and then they won us the League. It was a massive effort from Lee, and I really rate his contribution.

Denise and I are quite close to him and his wife, Leslie, and we've had any number of good nights out. He's a bit of a wine buff – too knowledgeable when it comes to my turn to pay – and he has a massive collection of some of the very best stuff. The four of us go to a pub called the Crab and Lobster a lot where the owners, Dave and Jackie Bernard, know what to expect when Chappy walks in.

We might have missed Lee's goals in recent times but I think that particular drought is over following the arrival of Tony Yeboah. It might have surprised a few people when Howard Wilkinson got him from Germany's Bundesliga but I had seen him on television a few times and knew roughly how good he was. The Ghanaian was a huge hit at Saarbrucken first and then Eintracht Frankfurt, and even in his fairly brief spell to date at Elland Road I'm one hundred per cent certain it will be the same here. The signs are good.

Howard protected him quite nicely when he arrived in Leeds last season and even though we weren't getting goals he kept him out of the starting line-ups because he knew his fitness was suspect. The prime example of that was a cup-tie against Manchester United at Old Trafford when everyone wanted him on from the beginning but the manager felt he wouldn't be capable of ninety minutes.

But he managed thirteen goals for us in sixteen games and is clearly a very special talent. You can see it in training where we have eight-a-side games and his finishing – he likes to pass the ball into the net – is special. Those thirteen goals have come from something like only fourteen chances, which tells you just how good he is. Tony calls them 'golden chances' and tells us if he gets one he'll score. I like that because if a team is getting goals it's always got a chance. Sometimes even when you're not playing well and you have a striker who can nick one he's worth his weight in gold – or goals. Tony's like that, and the lads were all delighted when he agreed a longer-term deal in the summer. I think he was a bit surprised at how good a reception he got at Elland Road after he had suffered some difficult times in Germany. But he seems to like it and I think he'll prove to be a big player for Leeds.

That's a roll of honour – or should that be dishonour! – of some of the players I have enjoyed working with at club level. But, really, I could make a book out of the others. Maybe I will!

CHAPTER NINE

Football's Not My Only Sport

Just about everyone has a sporting hero or two they admire above anyone else, and I'm no different. And since golf is one of my other great loves in life – apart from the family and football – I suppose it's only natural to turn there for one of my special idols.

Seve Ballesteros is a player I have always respected more than most. My first recollection of the Spaniard was back in 1976 when I was only eleven. He was playing at Royal Birkdale during that long, hot summer and he was fairly young himself. But he looked to me as if he just loved playing shots. He was like a young cavalier who didn't appear to want to be too technical about a game that can sometimes become like that. Instead, he just wanted to play. Everything was simple and brilliant and he had the kind of natural flair for the game that I love.

It all stemmed from a remarkable background where, as I understand it, he 'made' golf clubs from sticks he found on the beach near his home. He would use stones as balls and even got to the stage of digging holes and making his own course of sorts. That kind of dedication is fantastic and it showed Seve was always destined for great things. He led for three rounds of that Birkdale Open Championship even though he was only nineteen, and eventually finished second alongside Jack Nicklaus. No wonder he attracted my attention.

I've spent years since then watching the man who is

undoubtedly my favourite golfer. There are so many aspects of his game I admire – and envy! He has immense power yet such a delicate and deft touch, and that is a great gift. I was able to see him at first hand in 1985 when Ali Mauchlen and I hopped across the Midlands from Leicester to The Belfry where Britain and Europe battled it out against America for the Ryder Cup. There was a host of great golfers on display but Ballesteros was like a magnet. We followed him round the course, marvelling at his every shot. He was both impressive and intimidating to watch so I kind of pitied the top Americans who had to actually play against him. It was hard enough watching him. I remember when someone clicked a camera just as he was about to try and hole a crucial putt. Seve gave the poor guy a stare that nearly froze him to the spot. Ali actually ended up putting his hand over his son Ian's mouth in case he said something at the wrong moment. Seve had that kind of hold over people and if I have a sporting ambition left it is to play a round of golf with one of the true greats of the game.

One of my most prized possessions is a montage of photos of Seve which my good mate Howard Clark got autographed for me not so long ago. I look at it occasionally and wish I could play like him! And I can sometimes see myself repeating that marvellous moment of his when he punched the air in the direction of the four corners of the green after he won the Open at St Andrews. Moments like that are great moments in sport.

Basically, my sporting heroes make their chosen profession look easy. They are naturals at their game, and that is definitely the case with Willie Thorne. He is a wonderfully gifted snooker player and, because I spent so long in his home town of Leicester, I have followed his career closely. When I played for City I met up with Willie quite a few times and I've seen him rack up 147 more than once. I've even picked the balls out of the pockets and respotted them when he's done it. It's been disappointing that he's never really reached the level of consistency at tournament level that he's clearly been capable of.

Still on the green baize, it's impossible not to rate Jimmy White. I can't help but admire a guy who gets on with the game the way he does. He has so much flair and ability that he looks comfortable all the time and makes the game look so easy. But I know it's not! I enjoy snooker but guys like Willie, Jimmy and the rest of the top professionals are on a different plane.

One of the sports I enjoy watching more than playing is tennis but to me – and I admit I'm no expert – it seems as if a lot of the characters in the sport have disappeared in recent years. I personally liked John McEnroe, and no one could argue that he wasn't a character. Ilie Nastase was another player I had a lot of time for, and although both he and McEnroe were possibly a bit volatile, they helped raise the profile of the game and, for that matter, the appreciation of it. They seemed to me like experts. They looked as if they had a wonderful touch but at the same time could also turn on the power. And both were capable of making a racquet – sorry, racket. But I can handle that because sport needs its characters. They are people fans identify with and that's what it's all about. I think years ago the average person in the street could have hit you with the names of a variety of tennis players but I'm not so sure that that would be the case now – and that's a shame.

In the world of cricket I tend to drift back to Leicestershire and guys like David Gower and Nick Cook who both played for the county when I was around Filbert Street. A left-hander at golf looks, to me, a bit clumsy, yet a left-hander at cricket for some reason looks positively elegant – at least Gower did. But then again, maybe David wasn't truly representative of all left-handed batsmen because he was special. He always seemed to make the game look so easy as he blasted bowlers all around the ground. His effortless style is not shared by many. But it is an effort as I once discovered in the nets when I faced Paul Jarvis. There was me thinking I was about to smash him all over the place and, instead, I barely saw the ball as it flew past me and crashed against the stumps. I discovered then that cricket's a whole lot more difficult than it appears. And the guys who reach the top at cricket, as in other sports, spend hours on their technique. But I just suspect with Gower that most of his ability was a natural asset.

I got to know Nick Cook pretty well because he was a Leicester City fanatic. He tried to explain all the ins and outs of the game to me – remember, it's hardly the number-one pastime in Scotland – and in return I would get him tickets for football games. He used to phone me on a Friday night and get me to organise tickets for the next day's match at Plymouth or wherever. He was that keen. I still keep in touch with him and I managed to get a few international strips for him to use during his benefit year.

But the bottom line for me is that golf is far and away my favourite sport after football. I still play whenever possible and I have a single-figure handicap. Ever since I first played as a youngster I have been reasonably good at the game, and because I'm with a big football club I occasionally get the opportunity to play with the professionals. But in terms of nerves I would rather face a huge and hostile Old Trafford crowd than play alongside these guys. One of the most nerve-wracking moments of my life was standing on the first tee waiting to play alongside Sandy Lyle, and I have also played with Mark James and Howard Clark.

The Lyle occasion was the Dunhill Masters Pro-Am at Woburn and two other amateurs and I were out alongside the great man. There I was, waiting to play after Sandy and, of course, he didn't help the situation by sending his drive hurtling about a mile down the middle of the fairway. Talk about putting the pressure on. I was a wreck when I stood and looked down the avenue between the spectators. It was very intimidating to see the rows of fans and, for a fleeting moment, I wondered if I would kill someone! I don't know who was more frightened – them or me.

But it was a fantastic experience once I got past that first shot and Sandy was a pleasure to play with. It must drive the pros mental at times having to go out and play alongside bumbling amateurs, but he was very patient. And he was far more helpful than he needed to be because he advised on distances to the flag and club selections and so on.

But at the end of the round I was emotionally drained after spending the entire eighteen holes paranoid about making a fool of myself. And just as I thought it was safe to get back in the water, so to speak, Sandy led me down to the practice ground and gave me a few pointers. He had spotted some fairly major mistakes in my game during the round and he did his best to sort them out. I was very grateful for that – until he asked me to hit a few five-irons down the practice area to get my swing going. I was quite happy to do that until I saw, standing next door to me on my right, Bernhard Langer. It was bad enough knowing the great German was so close but when I looked to the other side, there were Nick Faldo and Jose-Maria Olazabal! I think my bottle went totally then. And all Sandy could offer me in the way of advice was: relax. I was like a fish out of water next to guys who have won the US Masters, Opens and between them every other golf tournament worthy of the name. And it showed with my first couple of efforts although, happily, I improved a bit.

But the whole thing was incredible. I'm used to playing in front of 40,000 screaming fans every week, yet here I was, reduced to a wobbly jelly in front of those golfing superstars. Maybe they would be the same if they had to go and play football at Elland Road or Highbury or wherever.

But being captain of Leeds United and Scotland does bring its advantages like that day because even though I was a wreck for most of it I wouldn't have missed it for the world. And there have been other occasions when being a fairly well-known footballer has allowed me to meet, and get to know well, other sportsmen and women. It's one of the many big plusses about my job. I'm fortunate to have met many of the sporting personalities whom millions of people would give their right arm to be introduced to. I'm fairly pally with Howard Clark, and lads like Mike Atherton and Philip de Freitas have joined Denise and I for meals on several occasions.

Ironically, one person I don't know that well – although we had a round of golf together in the summer – is Gary Lineker. We both have Leicester City backgrounds but our paths haven't crossed that much, yet he is someone I have tremendous admiration for. Gary's career was a remarkable one by any standards. He was a prolific goalscorer at all his clubs – City, Everton, Barcelona and Spurs, and he had an amazing track record for goals with England as well. I doubt very much if anyone will get near his efforts at either level again.

But there was so much more to Gary, if you're talking about heroes and idols. For a start, Link was a tremendous ambassador for the game. Throughout his career it seems everyone has wanted a piece of him either here in England, in Spain, in Japan where he finished, or around the world on his international trips. That can be quite a pressurised lifestyle, but he appears to have coped with it all brilliantly and I don't know anyone who has a bad word to say about him. I realise, of course, that he's been handsomely rewarded for what he's done, but I think when you look around at some of our other so-called football superstars, it is a label that sits comfortably on him.

And it doesn't look as if he's about to disappear from the public eye simply because he's stopped playing. Gary looks just as comfortable on television as he did when he was about to score any of his amazing tally of goals. And he's always got his 'Mr Nasty' advertisements to fall back on as well.

Gary and these others are some of the sportsmen I enjoy, or have enjoyed, watching over the years. And I think they've all given a massive amount to their chosen sport. Sure, they've taken a bit out as well, but this is a two-way street and I don't think many people would begrudge them the money they've made.

CHAPTER TEN

War of the Roses

Roses might well smell sweet but when it comes to the War of the Roses – Yorkshire against Lancashire – it's anything but. It's the white rose versus the red rose but there's nothing flowery about the occasion when Leeds United clash with Manchester United.

The two clubs seem to bring out the very worst in each other's supporters and although I've been at Elland Road for some time now – and also spent a few summers at Old Trafford when I was a youngster – no one has ever adequately explained the ill-feeling. Basically, I think it's a long-time rivalry between the two counties. And although it never needs much to fuel the fire, there have been a few incidents that have done just that.

Before I go into one or two of them, I have to say that when you live outside either area as I did when I was in Scotland or even Leicester you have no idea of what it's all about. It's a bit like someone south of the border trying to get to grips with the Old Firm hassle – Rangers and Celtic – in Scotland. Only the people involved seem to know – or care – what it's all about. And there's no doubt it can get very bitter and at times downright distasteful.

I reckon it came to prominence in recent times when the brilliant team of Billy Bremner's era in the late 1960s and early 1970s were in such hot competition with Manchester United. Some of the greatest names who have ever played for either club were around at the same time and the rivalry was fierce. Apart from Bremner, Leeds had people like Gary Sprake, Jack Charlton, Norman Hunter, Peter Lorimer and Johnny Giles among others. The Manchester United side of around the same time boasted fine players like George Best, Denis Law and Bobby Charlton, so I would imagine the rivalry at that level would have increased the temperature off the field.

I would say, though, that as far as I know, the players then never had any problems with each other apart from that healthy rivalry. And even now managers Alex Ferguson and Howard Wilkinson appear to get on fine. Certainly, the players of both the current teams have great respect for each other and none of the off-the-field problems get carried on to the pitch. It is a bit frustrating, though, that Fergie's team have had the upper hand in recent years! But it's the fans more than the two clubs who take it all too seriously, and that can make it quite difficult for players to be transferred between the two places. Joe Jordan and Gordon McQueen apparently caused a bit of a stir years ago when they left Elland Road for Old Trafford. On the other hand, I don't recall Gordon Strachan, who left Manchester United for us, ever having much of a problem.

Yet the most recent of all – Eric Cantona – got a terrible reception when he came back to Leeds to play and the atmosphere was dreadful. It was just about as hostile as I can remember it when Eric returned, and although there were allegations of spitting I don't think anything was ever proved. But it wasn't pleasant to be part of all that.

It's clearly not unknown for players to cross the great divide and they should be allowed to get on with it without that kind of abuse. Leeds fans should remember, too, that we have been linked with former Manchester United striker Mark Hughes a few times over recent seasons so they will not stop transfers between the clubs by their loutish behaviour.

The whole thing is very like Glasgow where the Rangers fans and the Celtic supporters are divided by religion and hurl insults at each other on a Saturday afternoon yet quite possibly go to work beside the weekend's 'enemy' on the Monday morning. I'm all for healthy and partisan support but not when it goes beyond that and on occasion the feeling between the people who follow the two Uniteds has left a lot to be desired.

But Cantona and any other incident aside, the worst moment of all for me was after the legendary Sir Matt Busby died. Sir Matt *was* Manchester United for so long. Yet a minority of our so-called supporters refused to obey a minute's silence to honour him when we were playing at Blackburn. The whole sorry affair was live on television as well, and I have never been so embarrassed as I was then to be part of Leeds United. It was a grotesque and disgraceful dishonour by a few to one of the men who have done more for football in this country than almost anyone else. I genuinely thought beforehand that the half-wits might manage sixty respectful seconds, but I was terribly wrong and, at the same time, terribly disillusioned. Normally I will defend Leeds United supporters to the end. Generally, they are fantastic and very often worth a goal of a start because of their tremendous backing. But on that pathetic occasion I couldn't defend some of them at all. Similarly, talk recently of death threats by a so-called Leeds fan against people at Old Trafford is despicable.

Nor could I defend Manchester United manager Alex Ferguson when he recently wrote: 'I almost wanted Howard Wilkinson's team to be relegated because of their fans.' That was stupid and inflammatory and I was surprised someone of Fergie's experience would say it. But it was just another example of the long-running feud that does neither club – management, players or fans – any good whatsoever.

CHAPTER ELEVEN

Disappointment in the Champions Cup

You don't very often see Ally McCoist stuck – or at least nearly stuck – for words. The Rangers striker is an ebullient, chirpy player who seldom lets anything or anyone get him down. Even when he was at his lowest and couldn't get a game for Rangers under Graeme Souness, his teammates have told me that publicly at least he was still the life and soul of the party. But I reckon I came as close as anyone ever has to dumbfounding him. The miracle moment happened in the famous 'Battle of Britain' between Leeds United and Rangers in the European Cup in 1992, but before I come to that remarkable moment of near-silence there is so much more to tell about a campaign that seemed ultimately to involve most of the country.

It kicked off in the September when we were drawn against Stuttgart, and Rangers, incidentally, were up against Lyngby from Denmark. At that time, of course, there was nothing to suggest our paths would cross in such a dramatic fashion. There was far too much drama to come even before we contemplated the second round. The German champions were obviously formidable opposition and they had a few players who were more than simply useful. Frontzeck, Strunz, Buchwald and Knup were just a few names known to most of the lads before the draw was even made. So we had a healthy respect for Stuttgart but I think even we were surprised by the outcome of the first leg over there. The Germans played very well and we just didn't play at all. Put together, it added up to a disastrous 3–0 defeat and a bitter lesson that continental football can still produce the goods in some style. We just didn't compete on the night and, as a result, we were well and truly turned over.

Most people, when they saw that result, thought a recovery was beyond Leeds, and even I must admit it looked a very difficult task to redress the balance. The Germans generally aren't like some other European teams who maybe don't travel well. So, basically, we were up against it for the return leg at Elland Road.

But, when the night came, the whole country seemed to be backing us and the ground must have seemed like a fairly uninviting place to Stuttgart. As it turned out, the game was the exact opposite of the one over there. This time we were magnificent and Stuttgart struggled and we won a marvellous match 4–1 with Speed, me, Cantona and Chapman getting the goals. It was a magnificent comeback and a fantastic result – but it was, of course, in vain because Stuttgart went through on the away-goals rule. And that was definitely hard to take in the circumstances. We had been counted out yet had responded in brilliant fashion, and to go out of the European Cup after a display like that was galling to say the least. Or at least we thought we had gone out.

But this was a competition full of highs and lows for Leeds from the first minute to the last, and the following day it emerged that the Germans had at one stage fielded four foreigners instead of the maximum of three. The dressing-room feeling was at first one of disbelief that any club of that stature could blunder so badly. And I think when we heard the news we didn't allow ourselves to believe it. It just seemed inconceivable – and to happen to Germans with their reputation for efficiency, seemed a bit unlikely. But that view soon disappeared when the news was confirmed. By then all the players, not unreasonably, thought that Stuttgart would inevitably be expelled from the competition for such a gross infringement of the rules and regulations.

But in our excitement we forgot just how powerful a nation Germany is. UEFA can be quite a political animal and countries with huge populations (and therefore massive television audiences) invariably have a lot of clout. And Stuttgart weren't about to be thrown out of the European Cup.

Leeds' lawyer Pete McCormack flew to a special meeting in Switzerland to try and thrash the whole thing out with UEFA and Stuttgart. Eventually, it was decided to award us the second leg on a 3–0 scoreline, thus necessitating a third match. Peter, in fact, returned from that meeting with the distinct impression that we were lucky to get that replay. But that certainly wasn't a view shared in this country and, unusually, Howard Wilkinson got himself involved in a bit of a war of words. We were staggered that they had been allowed to remain involved after such a major breach. It was a ridiculous 'mistake' for any club to make, let alone a club of Stuttgart's stature and experience. But I think the fact that they got themselves a third bite at the cherry proved just how strong an influence Germany has at that level of football. By then, too, we knew the second round draw, and the prospect of a meeting with Rangers was some incentive to finally see off Stuttgart.

But there was one aspect of it all that pleased the lads, even if the whole shooting match was deemed a bit of a joke. We were being handed the chance to play that third match at Barcelona and anyone in football worth his salt wants to play at the Nou Camp Stadium. It is one of the great stadia in the world and there was an instant appeal in the prospect of battling it out in such an arena. We also felt we would have the edge over the Germans after the doing we gave them at Elland Road, so although we could have done without the game we were very optimistic. I think the lads reckoned we had another point to prove.

But that shoot-out in Spain was all a bit unreal as it turned out. Rangers manager Walter Smith and a fair contingent of

Leeds fans were about the only people in the vast stadium and the Ibrox boss must have been delighted to get the opportunity to spy on his next opponents in a do-or-die situation like that. But there was no real atmosphere for the players and it was a bit like playing in a reserve game from that point of view.

We went into the match still smarting from the fact that Stuttgart had been handed another chance in a neutral venue when at the very least we felt they should have had to return to Elland Road for the one-off match. But, basically, we took over where we left off in that second game. Gordon Strachan scored a magnificent goal and substitute Carl Shutt, on for Cantona, got another late on while Golke scored for the Germans. We had actually outclassed Stuttgart from the beginning of the second leg and I must admit to a sense of great satisfaction after we finally went through 2–1. We really felt justice had been done – and been seen to be done.

The German players at least took the defeat quite well and I think deep down they maybe realised they were fortunate to get that opportunity. It obviously takes a decent team to win the Bundesliga but we proved considerably better and Lee Chapman, for instance, gave German international Guido Buchwald a hard time. But all that did was set up a second-round tie. Mind you, it was the Battle of Britain!

We had a big Premiership game before then against Sheffield United – a local derby – and we won that fairly comfortably but, to be honest, all eyes were on Europe. The game against Rangers attracted massive media hype and it was built up far more than even a normal European Cup tie. And although there is a long-held belief in England that Scottish football is sometimes a bit of a joke, no one at Elland Road was laughing. Many people south of the border don't rate football in the north but we were too professional to believe it would be anything other than bloody difficult. Why should we have thought it would be any other way? Rangers had some of the most talented players in Britain at Ibrox. Guys like Andy Goram,

Richard Gough, Ally McCoist and Mark Hateley had done it over and over again for club and country. No one at Leeds was under any illusions.

But when you thought about it all, it was a fascinating contest and it's little wonder it captured the nation's attention. It was all there for a spectacular two-leg tie. Appetites were whetted at the prospect of Chapman against Gough, Hateley and McCoist against Fairclough and Whyte, midfield battles involving myself, David Batty, Stuart McCall and Trevor Steven, and Cantona and Durrant on show. I could hardly wait – and there was an extra edge to the whole thing because Strach and I were Anglos and needed to produce against our countrymen. I was even more desperate because I knew many Scottish fans hadn't really seen much of me apart from my spell at Fir Park and as a right winger for Scotland. They had never seen me in my more central midfield role so I was determined to show what I could do there.

And, to be brutally frank, I really fancied our chances of getting through to the Champions League proper. Oh dear.

Strach felt more or less the same, and since he had had a love-hate relationship with Ibrox fans when he was at Aberdeen, he was relishing the prospect of going back to antagonise them all over again.

We watched videos of Rangers in action and it all helped build up the atmosphere for the first game at Ibrox. As if anyone needed to. By the time the game actually came around, everyone was on a high. The only drawback and disappointment about the entire proceedings was that it was home fans only at Ibrox and Elland Road. It was designated that way for safety reasons and I can understand that, but it's not good for the game as a whole to have just one set of supporters in a ground. The fans feed off each other and something is definitely missing when there are no visitors. Mind you, I managed to get a few tickets for friends courtesy of A. McCoist Esq. on condition, of course, that he got some for Elland Road. We weren't meant to but they were for family or close friends and everyone was warned to be on his or her best behaviour and be careful when they jumped up and down!

When we finally got to Scotland for the big game we stayed at Cameron House overlooking Loch Lomond, a quite magnificent and spectacular setting. But we trained at Dumbarton's Boghead, and I had to explain to the rest of the lads that although it was raining over Dumbarton and that a huge black cloud was constantly hovering over Boghead, it was nice weather everywhere else in Scotland. I don't think I've ever been to Boghead when it wasn't raining.

Still, it didn't harm the build-up and our only problem was a foot knock for David Batty. And I think even that eased when he had his first look at Ibrox when we went there to train. The boys were all very impressed with the stadium and I recall a few references to the fact that the dressing-room had nice clean tiles. Ours at Elland Road at the time were a bit grotty but, I hasten to add, they've since been replaced.

But on Wednesday, 21 October 1992, all the talking stopped and the action began. When we went out for our warm-up in front of 43,950 Rangers fans and about fifty well-disguised Leeds supporters, the atmosphere was electric. The Leeds players actually quite enjoyed it and when they returned to the dressing-room a few of them were whistling a well-known tune. A couple of the words from the song were 'no surrender' but they didn't know what it was all about and they had merely liked the tune. I didn't have the heart to put them straight.

And when we walked back out, the tension around Ibrox was almost palpable. The noise reached a crescendo and you knew, if for some bizarre reason you didn't before, that this was a game and a half. It was as big as they come. It was the championship of Britain and that involved a lot of pride and prestige. And when the referee blew his whistle to get it all in motion, the Ibrox fans found another notch in the volume control. Batts, Gary Speed and I just looked at one another in amazement. But there wasn't time to dwell on it. We had business to attend to – although we didn't for a second think we would attend to it in quite such a dramatic way.

There was less than a minute on the clock when we won a corner. It wasn't cleared properly and it headed in my direction. I knew even before it got to me that the only thing I could do was hit it on the volley. Sometimes that kind of effort ends up in Row Z of the stand; other times you catch it just right. This was one of the other times. The ball flew off my foot from well outside the eighteen-yard box and went past Andy Goram like an Exocet missile.

It's actually quite difficult to explain what happened next. One second Ibrox was a cacophony of noise and a sea of red, white and blue. The next it was like a funeral with not even a whisper to be heard. It was eerie. And it was such a contrast that I wasn't sure myself what to do! I thought initially that maybe the goal had been disallowed for some reason but no one had yet realised it. Or another thought that ran through my head was that maybe some supporter was on the pitch and that the game had been stopped. It was seriously unreal.

But then the lads, and the realisation of what I had done, hit me. I just hadn't believed anything could turn a frenzied, baying crowd of 44,000 into stunned disbelief. But I had and it was unquestionably one of the best goals I have ever scored.

That was magical enough but the fact that it came close to rendering Coisty speechless just put the icing on the cake! When I passed Ally on the way back for the restart I simply said: 'What about that for a strike then?' Normally Ally is as quick as a flash but it was obviously a fairly dismal moment and he didn't look best pleased when he admitted: 'I was meant to be picking you up at corners.'

His teammate and skipper Richard Gough later gave the Rangers version of the goal: 'In less than a minute our pre-match plans were put on hold and that huge, fanatical crowd had been silenced. It was an unreal moment, one of those instants which will stay with me forever. The cauldron of noise was suddenly hushed as my Scotland teammate Gary McAllister rifled in a long-range shot which beat Andy Goram – and which would have beaten any keeper – and ended in our net.

'It was the worst possible start, the worst kind of opening you can suffer in any European tie. In this one it seemed so much worse because of what was at stake for the club. We had a larger view of the clash than just that Battle of Britain tag because we knew we had flopped too often in Europe and that this season was the one where we had to try to put things right. To go out in the second round again was unthinkable. To go out to Leeds was now going to compound the embarrassment.'

Just as Rangers didn't plan on losing a goal like that, neither did we plan to score one. You can't legislate for circumstances but we aimed to take full advantage and for a spell we looked pretty good as Rangers tried to recover from the shock. We could sense the Ibrox fans turning on their team a bit and that was a sure sign we were doing our job.

But then fate took a hand and Rangers equalised in the only way they looked likely to – by a bizarre goal. The Scottish champions won a corner and, when the ball came over, keeper John Lukic lost it in the Ibrox floodlights and succeeded only in punching it into his own net. It was a crazy goal but it gave Rangers a lifeline and the crowd got going again after it. You could see their players growing in stature and confidence and, sure enough, McCoist scored to make it 2–1 at the interval. From being ahead and – relatively speaking – cruising, we were suddenly behind.

But I have watched that game any number of times and I still think more than ever that a Gordon Strachan effort that was ruled out for offside should have stood. Strach and Gary Speed played a good one-two through their defence and I didn't see much wrong with it. But it wasn't to be and, although the second half was played at a fever pitch with guys like Ian

Ferguson and Strach having one or two little altercations, there was no more scoring.

Probably if you had asked us before the start of that match, we would have been reasonably happy – or at least not too unhappy – to come away from Ibrox with a 2–1 defeat. But, having been ahead, we felt we had thrown it away a bit and that was disappointing. I didn't see any of the Rangers lads afterwards because we left quickly to get back down south, but they were reasonably pleased with their victory. They fancied their chances of getting through – but so did we.

And the English press were *very* confident that Leeds would make it to the Champions League. It seemed to them to be just a case of getting the Elland Road game over and done with and off we would go. But I was concerned about that attitude and a bit unhappy about it as well. I knew that Walter Smith would use the English newspaper reports to wind up the Ibrox lads for the return and I could just envisage him pinning some of the more confident predictions up on their noticeboard. As if it wasn't going to be difficult enough – and I knew that would be the case for sure.

The build-up to the return leg was much the same as before but, if possible, with even more hype. I had one quick chat with Coisty – about the ticket arrangements – but otherwise there was no contact and I don't think anyone would expect it any other way in the circumstances.

But we had a major problem going into the return. Batts, who had struggled to make the first game, was ruled out of the Elland Road clash. I think he would have been struggling anyway but a hefty Stewart Robson tackle in the Saturday game before the Rangers match – against Coventry – confirmed his absence. And to put the tin lid on that match I scored an own goal. So David Rocastle, who had played against Stuttgart in the game in Germany but wasn't a regular, came into the side. You really need all your big players for a game like that but Rocky was Leeds' record signing at £2 million, so we couldn't complain.

The situation that faced Rangers was the same as the one we had encountered in Glasgow, with just a smattering of their fans in an Elland Road packed with bodies and anticipation. It must have been just as mind-blowing for them as it was for us. And, but for a sequence of events, it could have got a whole lot worse for the 'Gers.

Almost as soon as the whistle blew to start the match we were off and running in Andy Goram's direction. Rocastle sent Eric Cantona bursting through the middle and for all the world it looked like being an even more spectacular start than it had been at Ibrox. The French star hesitated perhaps a second too long, but having said that I thought John Brown handled the ball and also bundled Eric off it in a double whammy that might just have got us a sensational start. Instead, Andy Goram smothered the ball and, really, that set the pattern because he was immense throughout.

But before we could build on that attack there was another of those extraordinary moments that will always be recalled by those who were at Elland Road that night. And, unfortunately, I remember it fairly clearly myself. Just about as quickly as I had scored at Ibrox, so Mark Hateley did it against us. It was an incredible coincidence – the kind I could have done without, really. I was immediately behind big Mark and, sadly, had a great view of the moment. He picked up the ball outside the penalty area and looked as if he was going to lob it back across the box. That's what John Lukic thought as well and, really, it was the only thought he could have had from the angle. But to our mutual horror, Mark chose instead to lash the ball towards goal – and it went in at the near post as Lukic tried frantically to keep it out. It was a stunning strike and, coming as early as it did in a carbon copy of my goal in Glasgow, it set us back on our heels for a bit.

We knew then we had a lot more to do but we still felt we had a real chance since a 2–1 win would have taken it to extra time. And, after all, Rangers had come back from losing that early goal to me to record that scoreline in the first game, so it certainly wasn't beyond us.

So for a while it was all about us pressing forward and the 'Gers countering whenever possible and, to be fair, making the occasional chance.

The Ibrox side were playing very well but no one more so than Andy Goram. The thought runs through your head when you see a keeper playing that way that you might never score and he certainly did his damnedest to make that true. He had an incredible night and I haven't seen too many performances better than his then. He seemed to stop everything we threw at him, and on the rare occasions he was beaten, someone like David Robertson or John Brown would pop up on the line. It was very frustrating for us and the fans.

And all the while Hateley, McCoist and Ian Durrant were making sure we couldn't throw everything forward because they broke cleverly and as often as possible to keep us on our toes at the back. Even our famed set-pieces were bringing no reward, and that was unusual. So at half-time manager Howard Wilkinson insisted we step up the pace even more and we felt if we could do that we were still in there with a shout.

But once again Rangers caught us short with a classically simple goal. We were up the park in numbers launching another blitz on Handy Andy when Rangers broke clear. Stuart McCall sent Hateley on his way down the left and the big man was an impressive athlete on the run like that. He gained a lot of ground before whipping over a great cross for McCoist to head home. Defensively, we were all over the place because the lads were all caught up the park. But credit to Rangers: it was a brilliant goal, even if I didn't think so at the time. I think it is one of the very few times Coisty has scored with a header! But he's never let me forget it, that's for sure, and I seem to recall him making some pointed remark at the time in answer to mine at Ibrox!

After that it became quite desperate and although we got a consolation goal late on through Cantona, it was only a token effort. I've watched the video of that game countless times since that night and I'm sure Goram pops up to make even more saves each time I view it. It really was an incredible performance from him and I think he did a lot that evening to make the English think twice about all the jokes – unwarranted – that used to surround Scottish goalkeepers.

And there's no doubt that Rangers' performance as a whole made people sit up and take note. It opened a few eyes in the south and there's no doubt they impressed many who had no idea about the standard beforehand. The club also made a lot of friends because they played so well. But at the time I definitely wasn't one of them.

I can't recall ever being so down after a match. It was bad enough to have crashed out of the European Cup but worse still to do so to my own countrymen. But even I didn't realise just what a hangover effect that defeat would have on Leeds. I remember losing the following game 4–0 to Manchester City at Maine Road, and it was all downhill from then. The Euro disaster really had a devastating impact, and our season crumbled badly. We could do little or nothing right simply because we couldn't shrug off the memory of the Rangers tie. We didn't win an away game all season, for instance, and we were the only side in the division to achieve that unfortunate distinction. It must also be unusual – maybe even unique – for the previous year's champions to go through a season without once winning away from home. But we struggled – and we struggled badly. There are other things you could put the whole sorry saga down to but for me the biggest factor by far was that desperate defeat. We just never recovered. It was as plain and simple as that.

Rangers, on the other hand, went from strength to strength. That victory put them in the Champions League – with all its attendant glory and riches – and they did well for Scotland in particular and Britain in general. Gary Speed and I actually travelled north to watch their first game against Marseille and that was another amazing Ibrox night. The French took the game by the scruff of the neck and they went 2–0 ahead going on five or six. Guys like Didier Deschamps and Abede Peli were actually toying with Rangers. But that all stopped when substitute Gary McSwegan sent a remarkable eighteen-yard header past their keeper and the place went absolutely mental when Hateley scrambled home the equaliser. We had a beer with the Rangers lads afterwards and they appreciated that we had come up. But they were also well aware they had got out of jail against Marseille.

I followed their involvement from a bit further afield after that and it was never less than eventful. They beat CSKA Moscow on a neutral ground in Germany because it was midwinter in Russia and then drew in Brugge. After that they beat the Belgians at home, drew in Marseille and drew again at home to CSKA. It meant, when you considered their two first-round games against Lyngby, that they had gone through an entire European Cup campaign unbeaten, which speaks volumes for their ability and determination. Yet they were pipped for a final spot by a point by Marseille, who went on to beat AC Milan before the roof caved in on their supremo Bernard Tapie and, indeed, the entire club.

Rangers took enormous confidence from the wins over us and, in fact, the entire campaign, and went on to win the domestic treble of Premier League, Skol Cup and Scottish Cup in an extraordinary season. They were on a high all the time and we were on a downer.

We managed to cobble together a few results like beating Arsenal and Blackburn Rovers, but it was a tense and fraught winter. We had some real horror shows. We were well beaten by Nottingham Forest, Spurs and even Norwich City, and had some fairly unexciting draws against the likes of Arsenal and Manchester United.

But we were scrapping for everything we could get – minus Eric Cantona who had gone to Old Trafford – and it needed a lot of determination to keep clear of relegation. We just made it by finishing seventeenth — or, if you prefer it, sixth bottom, just a couple of points away from the dreaded drop. It was ridiculous that champs one year could turn into chumps the next.

CHAPTER TWELVE

On the World Cup Rollercoaster

Scotland as a football nation remains an enigma. We can beat the best and lose to the worst. Being involved at international level is like being on a roller-coaster. I've always believed I've been in some highs and lows with my various clubs but they're nothing to the peaks and troughs you get with your country. Or, at least, with Scotland.

It's nothing particularly new, because all the great players of the past like Jim Baxter, Jimmy Johnstone, Willie Henderson, Kenny Dalglish, Graeme Souness and the countless others who have donned the dark-blue jersey have no doubt experienced the same ups and downs. But until you're part of it all I don't think you get an accurate picture. Sometimes that picture is an X-certificate, other times it's a weepy, but it's always an adventure and occasionally it's even a spectacular! But it's never dull.

Or, at least, I've never found it that way since I broke through after being virtually ignored at all the usual levels up to the senior side. Some lads, like Paul McStay for example, are brought through the ranks at just about every age-group. Others make the breakthrough without all that. I was one of the latter group although I did manage a 'B' game against what was then Yugoslavia, and one Under-21 cap as well, against Norway in 1990, as an over-age player. Just! And I could see the benefit of putting players in those games because Scotland under Andy

Roxburgh and Craig Brown like continuity. McStay, much more than me, has noticed that training for the Under-21s, for example, is very similar to the stuff you do at senior level. It's actually quite sensible because players moving up to the big team know what to expect.

I think the idea stems from Roxburgh and from the National Training Centre at Inverclyde in Largs. A lot of Scotland's managers and coaches go there for their badges and you can see the methods all through the game via what has become known as the 'Largs mafia'. I don't see too much wrong with that, to be honest, because I know for a fact that the Scottish coaching badge is much sought after. People come from all over the world to the summer courses and, when you analyse it, it didn't seem to do Roxburgh any harm. He is, after all, UEFA's top man on the coaching side. These efforts are often much maligned but like so many other aspects of Scottish life you sometimes have to leave the country to appreciate them. You really can be *too* close.

But that is a side issue here even if it's important to the development of our game. And those thoughts were a long way off when I was a bit younger and looking at my first Scotland appearance.

It was in 1990 when I was at Leicester City and although I felt I had played well enough previously when I was with Motherwell I never got a look-in. Maybe in England you are playing at a higher level and that certainly proved to be the catalyst to an international career for me. But whatever or wherever I was, it was a big honour, and although it's often knocked I still believe that.

So I got the call for the game against East Germany and even that was a bit unusual because I was drafted in after Jim Bett called off through injury. And from being nowhere in sight, all of a sudden I started practising all the free kicks and dead-ball situations. I was running the show! And I was loving every minute of being in among the big boys – although, remember, I wasn't just a novice at the game, I was twenty-five. I was just a late starter or late developer! I suppose one of my regrets is that I didn't get involved much earlier. But beggars can't be choosers and I was just happy to be there.

The side that day was: Andy Goram, Gary Gillespie, Murdo MacLeod, Craig Levein, Alex McLeish, Richard Gough, Gary McAllister, Stuart McCall, Gordon Durie, Maurice Johnston, John Collins. Substitutes: Paul McStay for Gillespie, Ally McCoist for Durie.

It was a decent team but not the most inspiring of debuts for me because we lost 1–0. There was one crumb of comfort, though, and that was the consolation of getting Thomas Doll's East Germany jersey. He was their best player and one of the few to make it into the all-German side after the Berlin Wall came down.

The games round about then were all part of the Scotland build-up to the World Cup finals in Italy, and although I hadn't kicked a ball for my country in the qualifying stages, I obviously now had a chance of going in the summer. That build-up continued with a game at Pittodrie against Egypt which, in view of the 3–1 defeat, I was probably quite happy to have missed!

But I was back in the frame for the next one against Poland in Glasgow and Andy Roxburgh continued trying things out before he settled on a line-up to kick-start the World Cup a month afterwards.

The Scotland side that drew 1–1 with the Poles courtesy of a Johnston goal was: Goram, Gough, Gillespie, Levein, Maurice Malpas, McCall, Roy Aitken, McAllister, MacLeod, Johnston, McCoist. Substitutes: Collins for MacLeod, Alan McInally for Johnston.

After that friendly things started to hot up in earnest and slap bang in the middle of it all I was conducting all the transfer talk that would eventually take me from Leicester to Leeds. But before that deal was done we went to Malta to acclimatise for Italy. And when we were there, apart from fitting in a game against the hosts, we did a massive amount of stamina work which seemed a bit strange after a long, hard season. And we weren't the only ones to think so.

Jackie Charlton's Eire squad were also in town for the same reason and they looked on incredulously from the sidelines as we grafted away in the heat. Andy felt we needed that kind of work but the Irish had an altogether more laid-back approach to it all. In actual fact, it got a bit boring in Malta although Roxburgh tried hard to mix things up to prevent that.

Groups of us went out at night with a senior member of staff just to break the monotony. One night it would be with Andy, then maybe Craig or Alan Hodgkinson and so on. Davie Cooper, Murdo MacLeod, Ally McCoist, Stuart McCall and I were in one group and, as you can imagine, there were a few laughs. Coop was still very much involved then and it was a real blow when he later withdrew through injury. And, of course, it was a dreadful shock to me when I heard earlier this year that he had died. He was a smashing lad although I didn't know him as well as many others. And he was an incredible player. I saw him for myself in training at that time and you couldn't help but admire his ability and, for that matter, admire him. He had been there, seen it and done it all previously, yet he still retained a tremendous enthusiasm for it all. He inspired so many of the younger lads by doing for Motherwell what Gordon Strachan later did for Leeds and what last season Jurgen Klinsmann did for Tottenham. He had that kind of aura about him that only comes from being a first-class professional. World-class players don't let their standards drop and that was Davie all over. It was a big blow when he withdrew because I'm absolutely convinced he would have been a star attraction in Italy. The World Cup finals – especially in a country where they admire their football so much – would have been the perfect stage for him. And he might very well have been the difference as far as Scotland was concerned. But that's jumping the gun a bit.

Our game in Malta was a worthwhile exercise and we won

2–1 thanks to an Alan McInally double. The team for the last outing before the serious stuff was: Goram, Gough, Aitken, Dave McPherson, Gillespie, McStay, McCall, Bett, Malpas, Johnston, McInally. Substitutes: Jim Leighton for Goram, Craig Levein for Gillespie, Collins for McStay, McAllister for Bett, McCoist for Johnston.

When all that was over, though, we weren't too unhappy to get back home for a brief spell. There was a lot to do even then before we headed off once more for the World Cup itself. I made my move for one thing and I was quite happy to get that all resolved and out of the way before Italy. So I left the lads as a Leicester City player and rejoined them as a Leeds United player. No wonder they were confused!

When we teamed up again we all got kitted out with blazers, flannels, shirts and shoes, and if there is one thing the Scottish Football Association do particularly well it's making sure you look the part. In fact, although they are heavily and regularly criticised for just about everything, the players never want for anything and from a morale point of view that is good.

But getting loads of gear did have its awkward moments when we picked up our leisure wear and training stuff once we got to Italy. A few of the lads were on individual contracts with different sportswear manufacturers and when all the Umbro stuff was handed over there were a few murmurings of discontent. I was with Lotto, for example, and I think Mo Johnston was with Puma, for instance. But the SFA's contract with Umbro meant we had all to wear their gear and that was that. I think eventually my family were the best-kitted-out people anywhere and they were certainly walking advertisements for Umbro! But that was only a minor inconvenience and no more than a hiccup in the overall scheme of things.

There was some serious concern, though, over the training facilities in Italy. Andy Roxburgh, thorough as ever, had taken the squad across to Italy a few months previously to have a look around at the set-up for the summer. It was also used as a goodwill gesture to try and win over the local fans and we all went along to the big local derby between Genoa and Sampdoria and were introduced to the crowd. We had a good look at the impressive Luigi Ferraris Stadium where we were to meet Costa Rica and Sweden, and we also took the opportunity to go to Rapallo to see our training headquarters. It was a toilet. We couldn't believe it and remained a bit sceptical when locals assured us it would be fine by the summer. So there were a few misgivings among the lads when we got there for the second time, but the local people had been right. It was absolutely immaculate. Players generally like to have a moan about everything and anything, but on this occasion they couldn't find much to complain about. The training facilities were first-rate and the Hotel Bristol in Rapallo where the squad was based was the perfect place.

Well, it was near-perfect, but there again they couldn't do anything about the fact that I was rooming with Stuart McCall. Our careers have run parallel in some ways and, certainly, we have roughly the same number of caps after starting at more or less the same time.

So it wasn't really too bad and it wasn't long before we settled down and started to enjoy the buzz that goes hand in hand with a World Cup. The media attention from the Scottish and foreign press was incredible and that, along with the occasional visit from members of the Tartan Army, gave everything just the right atmosphere.

But it was a seriously expensive place to be. We had an allowance of £40 a day and you needed it just to buy the occasional coffee when we took a stroll into Rapallo. We got out and about like that whenever possible and it really is a lovely part of the world. I could quite easily live there if it wasn't for the high cost of living.

We weren't on holiday, though, and we worked hard in training to try and make sure we were ready for the opening game against Costa Rica. By then I was thinking that Andy

Roxburgh knew the team he wanted to put out in that vital opener – and I didn't think I was about to be included. It was disappointing and I didn't readily accept it because I always wanted to play. But deep down I realised that I had only two caps and guys like Roy Aitken, Jim Bett, Maurice Johnston and others had been there before and had all the experience in the world.

So when the team was confirmed I wasn't that surprised although there was some astonishment over the fact that Ally McCoist wasn't playing. He himself tells a great story of the moment he discovered, to his horror and embarrassment, that he was missing out. Roxburgh apparently pulled the five strikers in the squad – Ally, Mo, Alan McInally, Robert Fleck and Gordon Durie – to one side and told them he was playing two up front – Mo 'n' Ally. At least it sounded like good news to Coisty and he was happy till Andy next referred to Mo and big Alan and Coisty realised he had earlier said Mo and Nally – which was an abbreviation of McInally! And that certainly wiped the smile off Ally's face although with me not even on the bench I couldn't raise much of a laugh either. That's the way it is at times like that because a quart doesn't fit into a pint pot, or, in this case, a manager can't play all twenty-two players in just eleven positions.

But while I was sorry for Ally I was pleased for Alan, the man who had become known as the Prince of Darkness because he kept slicking back his gelled-up hair. The name seemed to suit him. And when you've been together for days you get away with calling anyone anything. With guys like the Prince, Alex McLeish, Roy Aitken, Mo and Coisty about, no one needs to have too thin a skin anyway. There's never a dull moment in their company. And with younger lads like John Collins, Dave McPherson and Robert Fleck about the place as well, it was a good mix – which it needed to be.

But maybe Scotland should have headed home at that point when everything was going swimmingly, because we drowned when it all got serious. It was painful watching the side against Costa Rica. We lost a bad goal and, try as we might, we just couldn't score. It was, by any standards, a horror start. Yet in many ways it was so typically Scottish. We had arrived in Genoa with high hopes and almost before the competition had started we were struggling against all the odds. How come I feel I've heard that before?

The players who played in the Luigi Ferraris Stadium that day were devastated, and those who didn't weren't all that far behind. We knew we had blown a great opportunity to start in style and I don't think in our worst nightmares we had envisaged being beaten. But there was no turning the clock back and we had to get on with it. While the lads who played had a couple of days off the rest of us got on with training, and despite the general gloom hanging over the place it was very enjoyable. I grew in confidence to the point where I felt I might have a chance for the game against Sweden because it was obvious to everyone that changes would have to be made.

But a couple of further incidents deflected everyone's attention from the matters in hand. First, Richard Gough headed home after coming off with an injury at half-time in the opening game. His return caused a massive fuss with all sorts of stories doing the rounds, but I wasn't an experienced enough member of the squad to get involved in all the politics. I did know, though, that Richard had been struggling for a while and that we were fairly well covered at the back so I couldn't quite understand all the fuss.

Then there was an incident involving Mo and Jim Bett and some champagne. The two lads, I'm convinced, were set up for that yet they ended up looking like bad guys. Whoever was responsible, it was a petty thing to do, and it was turned into a real drama when, in fact, it looked worse than it actually was.

On top of the opening defeat, these things all contrived to make things more difficult for Scotland. And there was still further uproar when Coisty was again left out of the Swedish match. He was very upset about that and made his feelings known to Roxburgh, which was unusual for Coisty. But he clearly felt he should have been playing and wasn't amused to find out he wasn't. Instead, Andy went for Mo and Flecky, who had been looking particularly sharp in training where the standards had remained high despite Costa Rica. Fleck apart, there were a few other changes in the side as Murdo MacLeod, Craig Levein and Gordon Durie all got a chance. But I didn't, although I did make the substitutes' bench, which was something.

And despite Costa Rica, Richard Gough and the Mo and Jazzer [Bett] incidents – or maybe even because of all that – we promptly went out and performed brilliantly. If there is a perverse way of doing something then I think the Scots will manage it, and that's exactly how it worked out in Italy. We were no-hopers, lost causes, called for everything after Costa Rica, yet ninety minutes later we were heroes. What was that about a rollercoaster?

It was a fabulous night in the Luigi Ferraris ground where the Swedish and Scottish fans mixed like long-lost friends and the stadium seemed to be a sea of colour. The atmosphere was terrific. And a 2–1 win was perfect. Stuart McCall scored first and then Mo showed lots of bottle to score from the penalty spot. Glenn Stromberg got one back for them but we held on to put ourselves back in the frame. It's amazing the difference a few days makes. And from being just about down and out, all of a sudden all we needed was a draw from our last section game. I say 'all' slightly tongue in cheek because waiting for us in Turin was Brazil.

We were all a bit sorry to leave Rapallo, where we had enjoyed some tremendous hospitality from the locals. Even to this day a few folk we met there still come along and watch Scotland games whenever possible, so we must have created a decent impression. But we had to pack up and go and, believe me, that's no easy task when you think of the bodies, the kit and all the other bits and pieces that have to be transported. But at least we went on a high and when we settled into our mountain retreat high above Turin we felt we were capable of getting the point we needed to progress.

The team to face the Brazilians changed a bit from the one that beat Sweden and the biggest surprise was the return of Coisty. He seemed to go from first choice to fifth choice to first again in the space of just a couple of weeks, so I think even he was a bit taken aback at getting the call. Stewart McKimmie was also in and Paul McStay played from the start as well, whilst I remained on the bench.

We started well and everything was looking good for a long time as we held our own fairly comfortably. Then I thought I would get my moment of glory, albeit at the expense of poor Murdo MacLeod who took a full-blooded free kick from Branco right in the coupon. It was a belter of a strike and poor Murdo didn't know if it was New York or New Year, Turin or Torquay. He tried hard to shake it off but I don't know about anything else – it was his head that looked as if it was about to be shaken off. What a clatter he took. As he was trying to decide where he was, Andy Roxburgh gave me the nod and told me to go and get warmed up.

It was a dream come true. I was about to taste some World Cup action and, to complete the picture, it was against Brazil in one of the most famous grounds on the planet. I headed down to the corner flag with my tracksuit already off and I was raring to go when, to my utter horror and consternation, I saw Murdo come off and Gary Gillespie go on. I couldn't believe it and I must admit I felt as if I had custard pie splattered all over my face. My dream had turned into an embarrassing nightmare. To make matters worse, the switch that had been made was a bit unnatural because Gary went into the back slot and Roy Aitken moved into the middle of the park. If I had gone on, the side would have been relatively undisturbed.

The final irony was that we lost a late goal to Muller and,

although I wasn't aware of it at the time, some people blamed Gary for being too slow to react after Jim Leighton had failed to hold a shot from Alemao. I was too upset anyway and the only explanation I got from Roxburgh was that he had gone for experience when he made the substitution.

That was it all over for me and I had gone through the tournament without kicking a ball in earnest when, to be frank, I thought I should have. So it was very disappointing. Bryan Gunn, John Collins and I were the only members of the squad not to play some part in the proceedings. We had nothing to show for it all and it was a long way to go and a long time to spend away from home for that. In fairness, I did enjoy seeing it all at first hand and there's no doubt I gained valuable experience, but like any other professional I would rather have played than watched.

And after that Brazilian game everyone simply crashed out and wanted to get home although even then we had a bit of a delay because, until the Republic of Ireland's draw with Holland the next night, we still had a mathematical chance of going through to the next stage.

When it was all over finally, I looked back on it with a mixture of pleasure and sadness. I was delighted to have been part of it all but not playing was sore. Over the piece, though, there had been very few real hassles. There had been minor altercations as I've already mentioned and otherwise there was a brief dispute over money when there was some disagreement over who got what. It centred on lads like Steve Nicol and Brian McClair who had played in the qualifying games but didn't go to the finals, but it was resolved very quickly.

Otherwise there was no real hassle over money and I have to say there never has been while I've been involved at international level. The cash you earn playing for your country is a bonus and that's not why you're doing it. Half the time you don't even know what you're getting. And I've never heard anyone ask either. The players I have been involved with have genuinely been more concerned about playing for their country and winning than they have about dosh. That might be a bit old-fashioned but it happens to be the way of things and it's surely something for a player to be named in a national squad. It means you're among the best players in your country and that has to count for something. It was the same in Italy or at any other big tournament like that when a player in the squad is one of the best twenty-two in the land.

On a different theme the fans, once again, were unbelievable in Genoa and Turin. The Tartan Army is something to behold when they're on the march. My dad was one of them in the Italian campaign and he should certainly have got a medal for his efforts. He was booked to fly out to a perfectly reasonable hotel in Genoa but eventually left Edinburgh Airport as a stand-by passenger because the travel agent hadn't left him the correct ticket. He ended up with this guy dressed in a tartan suit with the Lion Rampant draped over his shoulders – the whole works. When they arrived in Italy they found themselves in Rimini rather than Genoa and facing a four-hour coach journey to the games and then the same back. On top of that the supporters were occasionally treated like animals as they were shepherded here, there and everywhere. The night of the game in Turin the heavens opened and my dad ended up like a drowned rat. He ended up borrowing a pair of socks from Craig Levein's wife. I think what kept him, and others, going was the fact that the bottles of Fanta orange they had were made up of one-quarter orange and three-quarters vodka. The Tartan Army has its own World Cup really.

CHAPTER THIRTEEN

Tartan Army Special

The 1990 World Cup, if it did nothing else, whetted my appetite for a bigger involvement in the Scotland set-up and I spent my first summer as a Leeds United player eagerly awaiting a fresh start at both club and international level. I realised, as has happened often before, that a big competition like the one in Italy can mean the end of some careers and the beginning of others. It is a natural progression on the international scene, and although Andy Roxburgh was known for his loyalty to some players I felt he would also be ready to shake things up a bit. I was also well aware my move to Elland Road couldn't possibly do my chances any harm.

I read the script correctly because when the new season got under way things went well for me. Hard on the heels of the World Cup came the European Championships and the Scotland group was one I very much wanted to be involved in. We had drawn Switzerland, Bulgaria, Romania and San Marino, which probably wasn't the most glamorous section but I felt it gave us a real chance of making it to the finals in Sweden in 1992. Eastern European teams are notoriously difficult to beat, on their own patches especially, and there were signs even then that the Swiss were putting together a formidable side. San Marino, in theory at least, could be disregarded.

So we embarked on another long, arduous journey with an

opening game against the Romanians in Glasgow in the September following our Italian adventure. And, unlike in those World Cup finals, we got off to a flyer, the best possible start, as we saw off Romania 2–1. It wasn't a bad old result because they had taken the lead through Camataru and all their big guns were being paraded which gave us an indication of how important they realised the section opener was. Petrescu, Popescu, Lacatus, Hagi, Lupescu were all there and Raducioiu was just a substitute.

Our side was: Goram, McKimmie, Malpas, McAllister, Brian Irvine, McLeish, John Robertson, McStay, McCoist, MacLeod, Robert Connor. Substitutes: Pat Nevin for McAllister, Tom Boyd for Connor. Robbo sparked our comeback and Coisty grabbed the winner to get us off and running alongside Switzerland, who beat Bulgaria 2–0 in Geneva the same night.

When these Euro games start they tend to come thick and fast and the next one, against the Swiss, followed only a month later. Once more it was a big one as both countries had opened up with a win. Once more it was in Glasgow and once more also we won 2–1 with goals from Robbo and yours truly, who notched his first for Scotland.

Team: Goram, McKimmie, Steve Nicol, McCall, McPherson, McLeish, Robertson, McAllister, McCoist, MacLeod, Boyd. Substitutes: Collins for McAllister, Durie for Boyd.

It really was the perfect start because even that early the Swiss looked to be our main rivals yet they had managed just an Adrian Knup goal at Hampden, and the victory over them left us flying.

One month later we had our first taste of travel – to Sofia – and a meeting with Bulgaria. I must admit I thought we were on our way again when Coisty opened the scoring early on. Todorov managed a fairly late equaliser but even so we weren't unhappy with a point from the 1–1 draw.

Team: Goram, McKimmie, Malpas, Jim McInally, McPherson, Gillespie, Durie, McAllister, McCoist, McClair, Boyd. Substitute: Nevin for Durie.

That was it on the European Championship front until March. It was interesting that Brian McClair had been recalled; although he was never the Tartan Army's favourite, the rest of the players always appreciated what he did. And before we got going again in earnest we had a friendly at Hampden against the USSR. I was on the bench and that was about the only memorable thing about the game for me as we lost 1–0.

Team: Goram, Malpas, Nicol, McCall, Gough, McLeish, Strachan, Fleck, McCoist, McStay, Boyd. Substitutes: McAllister for McCall, McPherson for McLeish, Durie for Fleck, MacLeod for Boyd.

Then it was back to the big time although I was injured for the return game against Bulgaria. We drew 1–1 again with late goals from John Collins and Emil Kostadinov. You really have to win your home games in these tournaments but fortunately the Swiss also dropped a home point – to Romania – a few days later so there wasn't too much damage done.

We finished off our efforts for the season in the picturesque setting of the Serravalle Stadium where we met group minnows San Marino. We didn't exactly excel but came away with a goal from Gordon Durie and a Gordon Strachan penalty to give us a 2–0 victory.

Team: Goram, McKimmie, Nicol, McCall, McPherson, Malpas, Kevin Gallacher, Strachan, McClair, McAllister, Durie. Substitutes: Robertson for Nicol, Nevin for McClair. It was great to see wee Strach back in business but no real surprise in view of the way he had been playing all season.

At the start of the following season we had a big game in Berne against the Swiss and we all knew exactly how important that one was, so a 2–2 draw was acceptable. We got a bit of a runaround in the first half when Chapuisat and Hermann scored and there was another blow when Maurice Johnston was carried off after forty minutes to be replaced by me.

But we sorted things out at the interval and Andy Roxburgh made the point that if we could get one back then he wasn't sure the Swiss would react very well. That's exactly what happened as Gordon Durie snatched a goal straight after the restart and Coisty hit the equaliser late on. It was a very good point.

Team: Goram, McKimmie, Boyd, McPherson, Malpas, Strachan, McCall, Nicol, Johnston, Durie, McCoist. Substitutes: McClair for McKimmie, McAllister for Johnston.

So far, so good. Our unbeaten record left us in a strong position but the Swiss and the Romanians were still there and so, too, were Bulgaria, with San Marino pointless and hopeless.

Then we lost our only game in the campaign – to Romania in Bucharest and to a late Gheorghe Hagi penalty into the bargain. I'm not saying it's anything other than a coincidence, but I was missing again that night!

So it all went right to the wire with Scotland needing to beat San Marino at Hampden and even if we did that we were still left with the worry of how Romania would do against Bulgaria a week later. It was an incredible ending to a long haul. We saw off the group minnows with little or no trouble thanks to goals from Paul McStay, Richard Gough, Gordon Durie and Ally McCoist.

Team: Goram, McPherson, Malpas, McAllister, Gough, Levein, McCall, Robertson, McCoist, McStay, Durie. Substitutes: Johnston for McPherson, Gallacher for Levein.

That put us on eleven points with just the Sofia clash still to be played. And I think every Scottish heart sunk when Popescu put the Romanians ahead because victory for them could have seen them edge it in a complicated finale. But then Sirakov equalised for Bulgaria and that's how it finished, leaving us a point ahead of Romania and Switzerland, and two ahead of Bulgaria. It's amazing how you can celebrate a draw from so far away!

And then it was a case of Sweden here we come. We had qualified for the European Championship for the first time – no mean feat – and we couldn't wait.

As ever, though, you can't just arrive at the finals and presume to do the business, so our build-up began in the February when we played Northern Ireland. It's really just a case of getting the lads together and playing rather than having a six-month gap, and from that point of view it was worth while. We also won 1–0 courtesy of Coisty and the team was: Henry Smith, McKimmie, David Robertson, McPherson, Gough, Malpas, Strachan, McClair, McCoist, McAllister, Keith Wright. Substitutes: Durie for McKimmie, Collins for McClair, Gallacher for McCoist, John Robertson for Wright.

We then had another home outing against Finland and drew 1–1 with Paul McStay opening the scoring and Jari Litmanen equalising. Team: Goram, McKimmie, Boyd, Dave Bowman, McPherson, Malpas, Strachan, McStay, John Robertson, Collins, Durie. Substitutes: McAllister for Strachan, McCoist for Robertson.

That turned out to be wee Strach's last game for Scotland and there's a certain irony in the fact that I replaced my great pal. The wee man had another great season that year but had been troubled by a back injury, and although plenty of people pleaded with him not to quit international football – including me – he was determined. So we went into the final lap of our preparations for Sweden without one of our most influential players. But there seemed no way back for Gordon and you had to respect his wishes.

We then embarked on a much-criticised trip to America and Canada as the finals loomed closer. People had a go at that tour because it was felt that the squad had had a very hard season and were about to face extremely tough opponents in Sweden. But it was brilliant. The lads got together in a way that could never have been achieved otherwise. I think Andy Roxburgh had learned a lesson from our pre-Italy trip to Malta when we worked tremendously hard, because this was much more casual. Don't get me wrong: we did work, but not with the same intensity as that other occasion.

We also had a lot of laughs, which is always good for team spirit and morale. We spent a few days in Chicago when we first arrived in the States and a group of us went for a beer at the top of the John Hopkins Tower. That was heady enough because the bar was 96 floors up, but it was nothing compared to a couple of hours later. We had a cocktail contest with names going in a hat and drinks being allocated thereafter. I can't remember what mine was called but it was dynamite! Ally McCoist still reckons that drink was the sole reason for my decent performances in the finals! And who am I to argue?

Maybe it was a celebration for me because by then I was far more established in the squad than I had been in Italy and I knew, barring disasters, I would be going to Sweden. And, happily, disasters were in short supply on the trip. We travelled to Denver to play the United States in the famous Mile High Stadium. And even though it was boiling hot and we could barely breathe at that altitude we came away with a 1–0 victory after Pat Nevin scored a glorious goal very early on.

Team: Gordon Marshall, McKimmie, Alan McLaren, McStay, McPherson, Malpas, Nevin, McCall, McClair, McCoist, McAllister. Substitutes: Jim McInally for McStay, Derek Whyte for McPherson, Duncan Ferguson for Nevin, Dave Bowman for McCoist.

You'll see from that line-up that a couple of youngsters such as McLaren and Ferguson were involved and it was good to see them breaking through. Alan is an outstanding defender and his performances since then have assured him of a long international career.

Dunc is, well, Dunc. I had heard about him before that trip so I knew not to expect a big shy lad. I wasn't disappointed. He's a real character but there's nothing wrong with that, because every squad needs them. And with guys like Davie Cooper,

Maurice Johnston, Roy Aitken and Alex McLeish no longer involved, it was good to have him around. He's also a fair player, of course. In fact, he's an unbelievable talent and that North America tour was the ideal apprenticeship for him at that level. I had the same thing in Italy.

So it was all good fun in amongst the training and we were able to see a bit of Chicago and Denver, which is unusual, because normally when we're away we eat, sleep and train and, really, we could be anywhere. Groups of us went out and about and, although it's not good for our wives to know this, we actually quite enjoyed looking round the shops!

After Denver we were on our way again – to Toronto – and a game against Canada. I had spent a short time there when I was a toddler so it was nice to go back and look around places I couldn't really remember and it also gave me a chance to catch up with my dad's sister who lives there.

On the social side we also took in a baseball game between the Toronto Blue Jays and the Minnesota Twins. Brian Budd, a pal of Coisty, fixed it for us and although I wouldn't like to sit through one too often because it's so long and involved, it was a great experience. The game was held in the Skydome and that in itself was worth seeing. It's an incredible place. Mind you, it depends where you're sitting and that caused a few laughs. Ally's friend organised four seats in the equivalent of the directors' box and four in the general seating area, so we had to draw lots. Stuart McCall and Gordon Durie were among the 'losers' and I enjoyed giving them a cheery wave from my luxury seat.

A few of the lads also took the chance when they were in town of going on a helicopter ride to the Niagara Falls and others went to the top of the CN Tower which gives you a panoramic view over the city. It was the perfect preparation and when it came to match time we were well aware of our responsibilities.

Canada proved much tougher – literally – than the States

but I got a couple of goals (one a penalty) and Coisty got the other as we won 3–1.

Team: Smith, Boyd, McLaren, McStay, Gough, McPherson, Durie, McCall, Ferguson, McCoist, McAllister. Substitutes: Malpas for Durie, McKimmie for McCall, McClair for Ferguson. The whole exercise was a great success – and a slap in the face to those who had doubted the wisdom of it all.

But the knockers were in full cry once more when we rounded off our preparations with a game against Norway in Oslo. To be fair, it wasn't a great game but Norway were a much better team than some people back home thought and, indeed, they went on to prove that time and again later. We got some heavy flak for the 0–0 draw but we ignored it and concentrated on the job ahead.

Team: Goram, McLaren, Malpas, Gough, McPherson, Boyd, McCall, McStay, McClair, McCoist, McAllister. Substitutes: McKimmie for Malpas, Gallacher for McClair, Durie for McCoist, McInally for McAllister.

As ever, though, it's only the real thing that matters and it doesn't come any more real than a group that pitched us alongside Germany, Holland and the CIS. Yet I felt we could do well in those finals. The build-up had been good, we had a fair sprinkling of fine players and the team spirit was like it is at a club. The signs were encouraging and we had the Tartan Army, in all its technicolour glory, right behind us. I don't think our Swedish hosts knew what to make of hundreds of guys walking round their towns in these strange 'skirts'. But, as ever, the fans won over the locals and I think it's safe to say they shared a beer or several hundred gallons.

Our group began with a 1–1 draw between Germany and the CIS, which meant we opened against Holland in Gothenburg's Ullevi Stadium. The Dutch were among the favourites to win the tournament – and little wonder when you looked at names like Gullit, Bergkamp, Van Basten, Rijkaard and Koeman.

It had been suggested to us that we might have a slight height advantage and that we should make that count, but I have to say that when we lined up in the tunnel they looked pretty big to me, so we disregarded that before we even made the pitch. And I was still playing wide on the right of midfield which isn't my favourite position, nor do I believe it's where I play my most effective role. But Paul McStay, Brian McClair and Stuart McCall, who shared midfield with me, had all been around the scene a bit longer so I accepted it. As it turned out it was a pretty useful midfield during that competition.

We did lose to the Dutch eventually after Bergkamp scored late on but it was rough justice on us. I knew early on in the game that we weren't carrying any passengers and that we were quite solid so I felt we always had a chance. They didn't threaten us that much, because Richard Gough was marking Van Basten and he was doing it brilliantly. Gullitt looked a bit lively early on but we sorted that out and, generally, the worst result we were looking for was a draw. Then Bergkamp got his goal – a fairly fortuitous one – and they left the field very relieved it was all over. I just couldn't believe we had taken nothing out of it after putting so much into the game.

Team: Goram, Gough, McKimmie, McStay, Malpas, McPherson, Durie, McCall, McCoist, McClair, McAllister. Substitutes: Gallacher for McCoist, Ferguson for McClair. Rob Witschge's jersey certainly wasn't a lot to show for all our efforts.

After that opening disappointment we moved to Norr-koping where the fans seemed well settled even then. They had taken over the town but no one seemed to mind unduly and there was a great atmosphere about the place. I like to think the supporters sensed we had a good team spirit about us and they definitely knew we had given a good account of ourselves against a Dutch side ranked third or fourth in the world. So we were still in good spirits after that game although we were very aggrieved we hadn't taken anything from it.

We resolved to do better against Germany and we watched

a few videos of them to bring us up to date on their form. Their names, though, we knew well enough: Brehme, Kohler, Buchwald, Hassler, Riedle, Effenberg, Klinsmann and so on weren't exactly unknowns.

But when the time came we absolutely battered them. We took them apart for long spells. I missed a real chance when Paul McStay sent me clear. I thought I had done enough but Bodo Illgner saved well. Big Dave McPherson missed another and it became a catalogue of lost opportunities. Everyone went forward to have a go, and time after time Gough carved out chances because the Germans seemed incapable of handling him. They scrambled the ball off the line, they humped it anywhere and they defended as if their lives depended on it. All the while we played some fine football and we had top performers all over the park. Someone later told me I put in thirty-seven free kicks or corners during that ninety minutes but still we couldn't find a way through.

And, of course, the inevitable happened as first Riedle scored and then Effenberg with an effort that took a wicked deflection – that summed up our luck and killed the game. It was as big a travesty of a result as I have ever been involved with and it was hard to take. I got Andreas Brehme's jersey and after that I would have been quite content to disappear for the rest of the night. I was bitterly disappointed that we had lost and, for that matter, that we were out of the tournament. So I found the fans' adulation a bit hard to bear and it was even harder to go back out and applaud them. It wasn't that I didn't appreciate their support – far from it – but it didn't seem to me like a moment for something not far removed from a celebration.

Team: Goram, McKimmie, Malpas, Gough, McPherson, McStay, Durie, McCall, McClair, McCoist, McAllister. Substitutes: Nevin for Durie, Gallacher for McCoist.

Those two defeats, when we certainly deserved at least a couple of draws, were a bitter blow but, if anything, they made us even more determined to bow out of the competition on a high. We knew we owed it to ourselves and to the fans to beat the CIS in the last game.

But before we set about that task Andy Roxburgh discovered what I thought was a far better way of saying thank you to the fans for their support. We were heading back to the hotel after training one day when the coach took a turning off the main road. We had no idea what was happening until we came across what looked like a tented village. Roxy – how he hates that nickname – had decided we should pay the Tartan Army a visit. It was a great idea and the lads were delighted. When we pulled up at what was basically a campsite in the middle of a big field a few fans were having a kickabout and I don't think they could quite believe what they were seeing as we trooped off the bus. But the jungle drums started beating, and the campsite went from being nearly deserted one minute to a sea of bodies the next as word got about. Thousands of fans poured out of the tents – I still don't quite understand how they all fitted in – and came over for a chat. It was a good public relations exercise and the squad was more than happy to say thanks. And we realised more than ever then that we simply *had* to beat the CIS.

And we did that in some style, which was important. Paul McStay put us on our way early on and then Brian McClair got his first goal for Scotland which delighted him and pleased the rest of us as well because he got a lot of unfair stick. I finished them off with a penalty.

Team: Goram, McKimmie, Boyd, Gough, McPherson, McAllister, McStay, McCall, McClair, McCoist, Gallacher. Substitutes: McInally for McCoist, Nevin for Gallacher. Andy Roxburgh got a bit emotional after it was all over but, basically, he was a fan in the first instance and he just wanted to share the moment with the rest of the supporters.

And it *was* a good tournament for Scotland, even though we won only once. We gained a lot of credibility from our performances in Sweden and there were a lot of outstanding players who did their reputations a lot of good. Top of that list was undoubtedly Goughie. He was quite brilliant in the three games and I don't know whether or not he was trying to prove a point after his disappointment in the 1990 World Cup in Italy. Whatever the reason, he was outstanding and any club in the world would have been pleased to have him on that form. He came up against some of the greatest names in the game but coped superbly.

But when it was all over I did have one big wish – I would just like to qualify for the later stages of one of these tournaments sometime. It wasn't to be in either Italy or Sweden and it certainly wasn't to be in America. I would have been grateful simply to get to those World Cup finals in 1994. But we never looked like making it if the truth be known. It was a difficult group and it proved too much as we became the first Scotland side since 1970 not to qualify.

We were back in with Switzerland for the qualifiers and this time were also joined by Italy, Portugal, Malta and Estonia. What you need in a section like that is a good start. What we got was a bad one.

Hopes were really high after our efforts in Sweden and we went into that first game against Switzerland confident we could keep things going, but instead it all fell apart at the seams. We were actually looking like taking something from Berne until a late collapse, coupled with the sending-off of Gough, left us down and out on the receiving end of a 3–1 scoreline. Coisty got our goal.

Team: Goram, Gough, Malpas, McCall, Boyd, McPherson, Durie, McAllister, McCoist, McStay, McClair. Substitutes: Gallacher for Boyd, Durrant for McClair.

And by the end of 1992, after two more home games against Portugal and Italy, it was virtually all over. We drew both 0–0 and although in some ways those weren't bad results I've pointed out before that you simply must win home games if you are to have a reasonable chance of success at that level. We didn't and we paid the penalty.

Team v Portugal: Goram, Malpas, Boyd, McCall, Whyte, Levein, Gallacher, McStay, McCoist, McAllister, Collins. Substitutes: McClair for Gallacher, Durrant for Collins.

Team v Italy: Goram, McPherson, Malpas, McStay, McLaren, Whyte, Durie, McAllister, McCoist, Durrant, Boyd. Substitutes: Jess for Durie, Robertson for Durrant.

Italy and Switzerland were already going well by then – certainly better than us – and it was a bit of an uphill struggle.

We saw off Malta 3–0 at Ibrox the following February thanks to two goals from Coisty and one from Pat Nevin.

Team: Goram, McPherson, Boyd, McStay, McLeish, McLaren, Nevin, McAllister, McCoist, Collins, Jess. Substitutes: Robertson for McPherson, Ferguson for McAllister.

We were still in with a shout at that stage although it was going to be difficult but it became impossible after a disastrous night in Lisbon in the April. I missed it – maybe thankfully – as we crashed 5–0 and Coisty broke his leg. It was, apparently, as bad as the scoreline suggests and it effectively finished our slim hopes of making it to the States. And I also missed through injury the last two games of that season against Estonia home and away. We won them both comfortably – 3–0 over there and 3–1 at Pittodrie – but it was too late. We still had a few games to go the following season but it would have taken a miracle for us to make it, and miracles aren't too commonplace for the national side.

The next September we drew at home again – to the Swiss – with John Collins scoring and Bregy equalising.

Team: Gunn, McKimmie, Robertson, Bowman, Irvine, McAllister, Levein, Collins, Booth, Durie, Nevin. Substitutes: Phil O'Donnell for Bowman, Jess for Booth.

It was an unremarkable night but for two things. The first was that I was made captain for the first time at Pittodrie and the second was that it was Andy Roxburgh's last game in charge. He resigned a few days later having equalled the legendary Jock Stein's sixty-one games as boss but more importantly because I think he wanted someone else to be able to get some time in the remaining competitive World Cup qualifying fixtures to plan for the future. But before anyone had a chance to do that we had to go to Rome to meet Italy; we lost 3–1 there, although it wasn't by any means a bad Scottish performance.

Team: Gunn, McKimmie, McLaren, Irvine, Boyd, Bowman, Jess, McAllister, Gallacher, Durie, McCall. Substitutes: McStay for Bowman, Durrant for Jess.

Craig Brown was put in temporary charge of the country's team in Rome and then, just before our last qualifying match in Malta, he was handed the job on a permanent basis. We celebrated that decision by winning 2–0 in the Ta'Qali Stadium with goals from Billy McKinlay and Colin Hendry.

Team: Leighton, McLaren, Hendry, McKinnon, Irvine, Durrant, McAllister, McKinlay, Nevin, Ferguson, Gallacher. Substitutes: Boyd for Durrant, Booth for McKinlay.

And that was that. Italy topped the section closely followed by the Swiss with Portugal third and us fourth. We had given ourselves too much to do from early on, and dropped points at home against the top three sides killed us good and proper. It was a real blow not to be going to America, especially after Scotland's run of finals in the past. But we have no divine right to make it every four years and bigger and better nations than us have failed.

After that, there was nothing else for it than to arrange friendlies to keep the squad ticking over before the next European Championship challenge and there was an added significance about it all as Brown settled into the driving seat. The first of those games was against Holland back at the new-look Hampden, but a Bryàn Roy goal gave them the edge.

Team: Goram, McKimmie, McLaren, Hendry, Levein, Robertson, McCall, McStay, McAllister, Durie, Nevin. Substitutes: Boyd for Levein, Collins for Robertson, McKinlay for McStay, Jess for Nevin.

Then it was Austria in Vienna and the two Macs – John

McGinlay and Billy McKinlay – gave us a creditable 2–1 victory.

Team: Leighton, McKimmie, McLaren, Hendry, Irvine, Boyd, McKinlay, McAllister, Collins, McGinlay, Jess. Substitutes: Ian Ferguson for Boyd, McCall for Collins, Shearer for McGinlay, Nevin for Jess.

And finally that season we had a fairly unhappy night in Utrecht against the Dutch. Duncan Shearer got our consolation goal in a 3–1 defeat in what proved to be Ruud Gullit's last international.

Team: Leighton, Stevie Clarke, Hendry, Irvine, McKimmie, McCall, McKinlay, McAllister, Collins, McGinlay, Durie. Substitutes: Gunn for Leighton, Nevin for McKinlay, Ian Ferguson for Collins, Shearer for McGinlay, Jess for Durie.

CHAPTER FOURTEEN

Scottish Pride

There is no doubt nowadays that club football, both in Scotland and England, tends to be given more importance than the international scene. The big clubs like Leeds United, Manchester United, Liverpool, Newcastle and Rangers have big-money commitments in Europe and in some instances they have to take priority. That undoubtedly causes club v country conflict on occasion and I have to admit I don't know what the answer is to that problem.

What I do know is that I personally love playing for my country and although I know it sounds a bit patronising I don't do it for the money. I do it because I genuinely enjoy it. It actually sounds a bit old-fashioned even but it happens to be true and I would like to think the same applies to most of the guys I have played alongside in my international career. Maybe that's being a bit naïve but, as I've documented elsewhere in this book, I've never heard a player ask how much he's on for this international or that one. So cash isn't really a consideration – and nor should it be, because very few people are given the opportunity to represent their country and, when they are, it proves they are among the best at their chosen sport. I happen to think that means something.

And, generally speaking, I have absolutely no grievances over the way I've been treated since I joined the Scotland set-up. There have been plenty of ups and downs, of course, but that's only to be expected. But I do find it a bit frustrating that Scotland can compete with the very best as we did in the European Championships in Sweden yet lose to the likes of Costa Rica as we did at the World Cup finals in Italy. I would like us to be more consistent and I genuinely believe we are capable on our day of beating virtually any country in the world – all the big guns – but that's simply not good enough on its own. If we do that one day and then play as badly as we sometimes can against a lesser team, it defeats the whole object of it all. I don't expect Scotland – or anyone else – to be able to maintain a world-class standard all the time, but I think we can be more reliable than we have been in the past at times.

The reason for that inconsistency is in part down to the players, in part down to the management and in part down to the set-up we have in football in this country, where we are asked to play week in, week out at a very competitive level and yet are still expected to peak when it comes to internationals. It might sound easy to do but, believe me, it isn't. So there are faults on all sides and I don't necessarily expect them to be resolved in my time.

There's no way of knowing how much time I have left at international level anyway. I just want to make the most of it, however long it is, because I feel I'm still making up for lost time. I didn't win my first cap until I was in my mid-twenties and that is seriously late nowadays. When I did, I found myself playing out of position wide on the right of midfield for a long time. I'm not complaining now, as I didn't then, but I don't think my teammates, the management team of Andy Roxburgh and Craig Brown, or the Tartan Army saw me at my best. That was an early niggle in my Scotland career and so too was not playing in Italy during the 1990 World Cup finals.

There have been other niggles too. I always felt it was a bit unfair, for instance, to get just one cap at the end of a season – or a tournament – to cover all the games. I know people talk about so-and-so winning X amount of caps, but what they really mean is that that is the number of international appearances he has made, whereas the caps he has probably don't bear any relation to the other figure. That meant that I, for instance, had just a couple of caps to show for my first half-a-dozen games. I always felt it would be better to issue a cap for every game with the date on it and the opposition so players could look back at it and identify the match instantly. Originally, I think that was the routine until the Scottish Football Association, presumably for financial reasons, discontinued the practice. A while ago I suggested going back to the old way and I'm delighted to say that's what now happens. Craig Brown or Alex Miller will now hand out a player's cap before or, more usually, after a match.

And since I'm on my high horse there's another matter I would love to change. I much prefer 'Flower of Scotland' to 'Scotland the Brave' as our pre-match anthem and I think I can speak for the rest of the lads on that one as well. 'Scotland the Brave' just doesn't have the same effect, although it's still a proud moment when you hear it being played either at Hampden or in some foreign land. 'The Flower', though, gets the hairs on the back of your neck standing up and it's quite a feeling to hear it with the players, and of course the Tartan Army, giving it plenty. I always envy the Scotland rugby team before a match because of that and you can see the likes of Gavin Hastings and Craig Chalmers are right into it. I've spoken to Craig Brown about this in the past and we did change for one match before reverting back to 'Scotland the Brave'. I'm told 'The Flower' can be a bit politically insensitive – sending the English homeward to think again, etc. – but that doesn't stop Princess Anne belting it out at every rugby international! It's something I feel quite strongly about and although I know it won't necessarily make Scotland a better side it sure as hell wouldn't do any harm. I think the message is getting through at last on that complaint.

But these things make me sound like all I do is moan when it comes to Scotland affairs, while nothing could be further from the truth. Honest.

But just before I move on to all the positive aspects of life in a Scotland jersey – and there are many – there is one last point I would like to make. And since this is my book I'm going to make it!

It concerns Richard Gough and I am well aware those two words tend to cause a bit of a storm when mentioned in a Scotland context. I don't know all the ins and outs of his very public fall-out with former boss Andy Roxburgh, and I can't throw any light on the reasons why he has never played for his country since Craig Brown became manager. It's really not even my business. But I *do* think Richard could have played on for Scotland. He is a very good player, an experienced defender and a fit guy. We are not so well off for quality that we can discard it readily. We're simply not like some countries who can choose a squad from maybe sixty or seventy players. We have a much smaller number of candidates and I think Richard, even now, is one. He got out too early.

Anyway, now that's caused a stir, can I say that I want to be in each and every Scottish squad for the foreseeable future. I actually get very upset when I'm not named or have to withdraw through injury or whatever. *I love the involvement.* It's both a break from the routine of Premiership football and a chance to test yourself against, generally speaking, the very best players in the world.

Every time I line up it's special, but even more so since I was made captain. That is an honour that simply can't be bettered in the game no matter which medals you win or which trophies you hold aloft. I mean that. I was ecstatic when Andy Roxburgh made me skipper for the first time against Switzerland at Pittodrie, and it's meant just as much ever since. Craig Brown has retained me as captain and we have a fairly close relationship. He asks me about the players' needs and encourages the other lads to use me as a link to the management team. It seems to have worked quite well.

And on the park there's more to it than simply wearing an

Gary Speed and Tony Dorigo congratulate me after a goal for Leeds (© Daily Mirror)

Lee Chapman, Rod Wallace and I enjoy a goal-den moment (©Varley Picture Agency)

Party time as the United lads celebrate the Championship in traditional style
(© Yorkshire Evening Post)

Greece lightning! I was determined the Greeks wouldn't stand in Scotland's way
(© Daily Record)

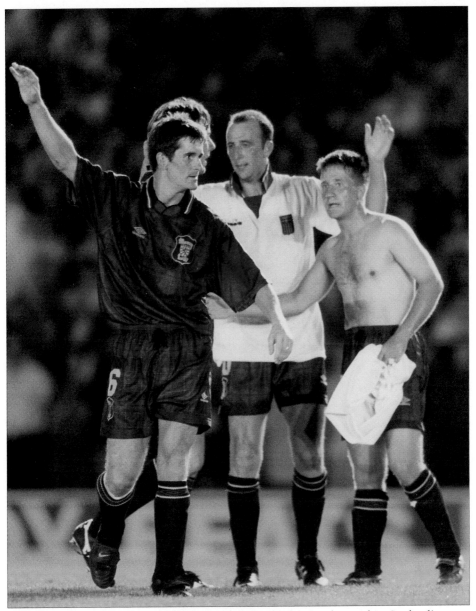

This is the moment the European Championship finals moved to within Scotland's grasp as I celebrate our victory over Greece at Hampden, alongside Tosh McKinlay, Craig Burley and John Robertson (© Daily Record)

Above: *In action for Scotland against Malta* (© Daily Record)

Right: *Not even veteran defender Franco Baresi can stop me in this match against Italy* (© Daily Record)

Left: *Me and my pal – I've learned a lot from Gordon Strachan over the years* (© Daily Record)

Below: *With my Scotland colleagues Billy McKinlay and John McGinlay – the three of us scored in a great win over Austria* (© Daily Record)

Above: *Just give me the ball, that's all I ask.*
Laying down the law in a Scotland training session
(© Daily Record)

Left: *Dreaming about that next goal . . .*
(© Daily Record)

armband. I am Craig's voice out there although sometimes in the heat of the battle I have to make decisions as well and I think he trusts me to do that. I have a certain licence to do what I think is right. If something requires instant change, for example, I will get on with it and Craig and his assistant, Alex Miller, can make whatever alterations they need to at half-time, or whenever they can.

The management–captain partnership is quite important on and off the pitch and, to be honest, I'm still learning the ropes as I go along. Gordon Strachan has helped me a lot, though. The wee man's been in the movie and he's said to me more than once that the best way to gain respect is to lead by example. It's not necessarily all about waving your fist or pointing the finger. Strach commanded respect – and plenty of it – by getting on the ball and doing the right things and that's something I've tried to do as well. Mind you, he wasn't above handing out the occasional rollicking but it was all about timing and that's something else I've taken on board. There are times and places and there's also the fact that you have to consider who you're dealing with. You can have a go at some players but you can't at others. It's all about knowing your teammates.

And when you're working closely with all sorts of people in a tight-knit group you have to know your manager as well. I've only ever worked with two at Scotland level – Andy and Craig. Andy gave me my first cap so I'll always be grateful to him for that. I think he had problems from some quarters because he wasn't a household name to start with and also because he hadn't played or managed at a particularly high level before he got the Scotland job. That was always, rightly or wrongly, going to leave him open to criticism. But when you look back and analyse his record, it wasn't bad. In fact, I think it might even have been similar to Jock Stein's – which must mean something. Remember, too, he was for a while the only manager who was able to boast of taking us to the European Championship finals.

I enjoyed working with Andy and we got on well. He's a

bubbly guy and loves his football. I never had a serious problem with him. For the most part his training methods were good and although players always find something to grumble about – it's part of our nature – you would be struggling to fault his organisation. He tried very hard to make sure monotony, which is always a player's greatest enemy, never set in, and although he was criticised for organising games and stuff like that, it helped pass away a few otherwise boring hours. He also knew our opponents inside out – he was meticulous about that.

Importantly, too, he had time for the kids, which was no doubt due to his SFA background. Whatever the reason, he always ensured the senior squad spent half-an-hour with youngsters doing a bit of coaching whenever it was possible. He was very keen to have kids coming through, and that's surely no bad thing. So, overall, I had no real cause for complaint with Andy. To reach the position he has now with UEFA would surely indicate he knows something about the game.

Craig became the almost automatic successor to Andy and that was greeted with some criticism as well, basically for the same reasons as Roxburgh's appointment was less than enthusiastically received. From the players' point of view, though, it meant that there was unlikely to be drastic changes because Andy and Craig had worked for so long together that their ideas had to be similar. And I think from the SFA standpoint it meant some continuity.

Craig, though, wanted to stamp his own personality on the job when he took over and he made a few decisions that suggested he was going to be his own man. He refused to reinstate Richard Gough, for instance, and he dropped Paul McStay which was totally unexpected. I'm not suggesting either decision was simply to make a point but they showed that he can be as single-minded as the best of them.

We have a fairly open camp but if Craig wants something done it will be done, although he also positively welcomes others' opinions. For example, we used to train every matchday but not all the players liked that because it was a change to their club routine where they rested on the day of a game. Craig accepts that and now we have a choice. If you want to go and do a stint to loosen up a bit you can. If you don't want to there's no problem. I think Craig realises he is dealing with grown men at the top of their profession, and as such they can't be mugs. He respects that.

And through the European Championship campaign that has been going on for the last eighteen months or so he has had Alex Miller by his side. I didn't know too much about Alex before he joined the squad as Broon's number two, but I've been very impressed with him at home and abroad through the qualifying run. He is very influential — maybe more so than people outside realise — and he and Craig work very well together. It's a good managerial partnership. They clearly talk about each and every aspect of their own squad, of the opposition and of the game in general.

They're not above listening to others either, because the Scotland squad has had a few 'guests' with us on trips over the last couple of years. Club managers like Alex Totten of Kilmarnock, Walter Smith of Rangers, Celtic's Tommy Burns and Alex McLeish of Motherwell are among those who have come along, and not just for the ride. Their suggestions are welcomed and they join us at training sessions where they express their points of view freely. Big Eck, in fact, is also involved with the Under-21 side alongside Tommy Craig. I think it's a good idea to listen to different people and different ideas because these managers have a wealth of experience of their own and it shouldn't be cast aside.

These guys were all doing their bit to try and get us through to the 1996 European Championship finals in England. They all deserve some credit for us achieving that target at the end of a long, difficult campaign. We have not been found wanting for effort, skill or determination and it has been a remarkable achievement to qualify once more. The squad that has battled through the qualifying campaign has been a pleasure to work with. It started away back last September when we had an eventful trip to Helsinki to meet Finland. In fact, that kind of paved the way for the whole thing because this seems to have been quite an eventful campaign one way or another.

That trip to Finland was memorable both for the excellent victory we had in the Olympic Stadium and the burglary we suffered beforehand! I must say it wasn't the best of omens to return from training one day and find a fair bit of your gear gone. A few of the lads were victims of a sneak thief and it's just as well we didn't disturb him or we wouldn't have been talking burglary here – it would have been murder, he wrote! It was a bit annoying to say the least. To be fair, it was the inconvenience more than anything else. The thief only took money and credit cards and even left Stuart McCall's watch behind. It must have been a Mickey Mouse one. Bryan Gunn, Craig Levein, Stewart McKimmie, Stuart and I all lost something simply because we had put our keys down at what we thought was a reception area – but turned out not to be. The funny thing was that the SFA security adviser did the same thing and then realised his mistake. He picked up his key again but left ours – he took some stick afterwards. He's been called Inspector Clouseau and Taggart ever since. He was slaughtered by the boys.

The worst thing from my point of view – or maybe the best – was that my wife Denise was in Paris with a friend at the time and she was trying to use the credit cards, which I cancelled immediately we discovered the robbery. I don't think she was too pleased when shops and restaurants refused to accept them. Ironically, I got the cards back a couple of months later but, of course, they were no use then.

The lads were all reimbursed for the money they lost. It was strange how we were all carrying £10,000 with us at the time – or so we told the SFA.

On the football front, meanwhile, we knew the

importance of starting the campaign well. A good result in the opening game of any qualifying tournament is vital and we were all up for it in Helsinki. I sensed after just ten minutes that we weren't in any real danger. I looked around and the lads were all looking bright and sharp. We knew they had only one player — Jari Litmanen — of real quality. The striker plays for Ajax and scores a lot of goals for them, so he was obviously a threat. So Alan McLaren marked him tightly. A few hefty slaps from Al early on unsettled Litmanen and took care of that threat. We went on to win fairly easily. Duncan Shearer scored a fine goal after a tremendous build-up and John Collins also struck for us in a comfortable 2–0 victory.

Team: Goram, McKimmie, Hendry, Levein, Boyd, McStay, McLaren, McAllister, Collins, Walker, Shearer. Substitutes: McCall for Levein, Jess for Walker.

After that, it was the Faroe Islands — we won 5–1 without me — and then Russia at home. We knew that would be a difficult ninety minutes because they looked to have a fair team. Andrei Kanchelskis, then of Manchester United, was in the side and I was a bit concerned about him; he has always given Leeds a hard time even though we have Tony Dorigo, an outstanding full-back. But Tom Boyd, as he had done previously, played Andrei really well, and although they produced a lot of nice football, we came away with a 1–1 draw. Scott Booth opened the scoring after I put him through and if we had held on to that lead for longer, we might have won. But they hit back quickly and a draw was probably about right.

In the build-up to that game I roomed with Brian Martin; it makes sense to have an experienced member of the squad alongside someone there for the first time.

The one unusual thing about our preparations was the fact that we heard from the Russian camp at Cameron House that the players there didn't have anything to eat after breakfast on the day of the game. It's a long time to go without food and a bit unusual to say the least. But they weren't a bad side nevertheless.

Team: Goram, McKimmie, Levein, McLaren, Boyd, McKinlay, McCall, McAllister, Collins, McGinlay, Booth. Substitutes: Nevin for McKinlay, Spencer for McGinlay.

We then had Greece in Athens just a week or so before Christmas and, again, we knew that would be a tough match. We went to Malta beforehand but that was a bit of a waste of time as it turned out. The weather there was poor and, unlike a previous visit, the training facilities weren't that good. There's also not a lot to do on the island and, to be honest, I think that the lads were quite grateful to get away to Athens and get on with the job when the time came.

But nothing ran that smoothly during the campaign and there was another hiccup to overcome before we even got as far as our hotel in the Greek capital. When our luggage appeared in front of us at Athens Airport it was quite clear it had been tampered with somewhere between the plane and the terminal. That was outrageous and it could well have been a bit of the old dirty tricks job by the Greeks. That kind of thing used to happen a lot as the home country, by hook or by crook, tried to unsettle the visitors by making life just as awkward as they could. I don't know if that was the case in Athens, but it all certainly held us up a bit. SFA chief executive Jim Farry was as hyper as I've ever seen him as he 'went to war' over the missing stuff. There were a lot of raised voices as the dispute continued. For some reason, it was mainly the young lads' luggage that had been targeted, but there was a fair bit missing and clearly that was unacceptable.

These events might all have disturbed us but for one thing the Greeks didn't reckon on: John Spencer. They would have had to nick the wee man himself to make a dent in our confidence, because he was in great form during the airport delay. It was vintage Spenny. He was at his irrepressible best. No one escaped his abuse and at one point or another everyone took some stick. The rest of the lads were all given pelters and one of the media boys was given terrible abuse because his trousers were a little bit on the short side. 'Has the cat died?' shouted

Spenny. 'Or are they long shorts or short longs?' The wee man kept us going through what seemed an interminable wait as Farry and the Greek authorities tried to resolve the problem.

Maybe that unfortunate incident – deliberate or accidental, who can tell – was a foretaste for the rest of the trip. We stayed in the same hotel as Rangers had for their European tie against AEK Athens, and that was fine. What wasn't fine, though, was the weather, and on the morning of the match there was *snow* on the hotel lawn. Goodness knows when the locals had last seen snow, but it certainly caused a stir.

Yet, even after all that, we went to the Olympic Stadium very confident about getting a result. There are times, however, when the gods seem to conspire against you, and this was undoubtedly one of them. We lost a bad goal to a penalty that, to be honest, I would have been looking for at home. It was maybe a harsh decision and we were all a bit aggrieved at the time but, as I say, I would have been the first to claim if a similar incident had happened at Hampden. Then, late on, we had a penalty claim turned down for an incident that was just as worthy of a spot kick as the previous one. But again the decision went against us as the referee, who was having his last international, 'celebrated' the occasion. In Glasgow, we might have got both decisions. In Athens we got neither and lost 1–0.

Team: Goram, McKimmie, McLaren, Hendry, Boyd, McKinlay, McCall, McAllister, Collins, McGinlay, D. Ferguson. Substitutes: Spencer for McKinlay, Leighton for Goram.

That was a major downer for us all and a particularly hard one to take. But we had to get on with it, and with Russia next in line, we knew we couldn't let the heads drop.

So we headed for Moscow quietly determined to get something to keep us on track. I must confess I was looking forward both to the visit and the game because I had never been to the Russian capital before and it was a chance to see the place as well, I hoped, as record a good result. I was happy enough with one half of that equation, but Moscow itself was the disappointment. The hotel was fine because it was German-built but the city was a real let-down. Maybe I expected too much of Moscow after all I had seen or read about the place. I just know it didn't live up to my expectations. Some of the poverty we saw on the streets would have made you weep. It's a city of astonishing contrasts now. One minute you would be looking at a luxurious top-class hotel which was either German or American-built; the next you would see beggars on the street corners. It was very difficult to come to terms with the whole thing and it wasn't at all what I had expected.

There were safety considerations as well, and we were well warned to stay in or around our hotel. When we did venture out it was as a group and at one point we went in the coach to Red Square. Again, I was a bit disappointed. I'm not really sure what I had hoped for, but it was a bit of an anti-climax when I actually saw the place for myself.

It was clear, though, that football is as popular in Russia as it is everywhere else, and we stumbled across a few locals with Leeds, Manchester United and Rangers tops on who were quick to ask for autographs. They also had all the soccer magazines and I saw some photographs of myself I had never seen before, which had to be duly autographed as well. And those youngsters would be standing in their football strips not in the least bothered that it must have been below freezing!

If Red Square was disappointing, the pitch at the stadium was absolutely disgraceful – certainly the worst I've ever played on at international level. The problem for the Russians was that the grass had been under several inches of snow throughout most of the winter and had simply died, leaving the whole area looking a bit bare and the worse for wear. It wasn't the kind of surface you're looking for in such a big game, but maybe it didn't do the Russians any favours either. They liked to push the ball about as they did at Hampden but that was no easy task on that pitch.

We also worked them much better than we had done in the

home game. We never gave them a chance to settle and play the way they wanted and instead of drawing 0–0 – a useful result – we probably should have won the match. Tom Boyd had a couple of great chances early on which, with respect to the Celt, might have been buried if they had fallen to a striker rather than a full-back. But Tom, in fact, had an exceptional night and it didn't take me long to realise we were up for a result. Colin Calderwood came into the side for a difficult debut over there and he, too, did well. The Tottenham player started out pretty late on the international road but no one could argue with the fact that he has looked the part.

Team in Moscow: Leighton, Calderwood, Hendry, McLaren, McKimmie, McStay, McAllister, Collins, Boyd, McGinlay, Darren Jackson. Substitutes: Shearer for Jackson, McKinlay for McGinlay.

The next venue was the Serravalle Stadium in San Marino, which has become almost an annual pilgrimage for Scotland. They are better organised now than they were the first time we visited but they still have no intention of trying to make a game of it, and that attitude brings its own problems for any opposition. The one way you can beat a defensive side like that is to run through them and we opened the scoring with a classic demonstration of that tactic. If it had been Romario who scored the goal it would have been hailed as a masterpiece and it would have been seen incessantly on television. As it was, it was John Collins who picked the ball up inside our half, meandered through a series of San Marino tackles and then planted the ball past their keeper. It was an astonishing effort and was one of the genuinely great goals. Along with a Calderwood effort, it let the Scots ease through 2–0, which isn't fantastic but is just about acceptable.

Team: Leighton, Hendry, Calderwood, McLaren, Boyd, Nevin, Jackson, McAllister, Collins, McGinlay, Shearer. Substitutes: Spencer for Shearer, McKinlay for Nevin.

The lads then duly went to the Faroes – without me

because of an operation – and completed the season's efforts in Europe with another 2–0 victory. I'm told it was a bizarre occasion. The squad travelled by bus, plane and ferry to get to the Islands and I've taken a bit of stick for missing it. But believe it or not, I would have liked to have been there. I'm hungry for as many international caps as I can muster and every game I don't make is, to me, a wasted opportunity.

So I was happy to be back in business at the start of this season and the renewal of Euro hostilities when the Greeks came to Glasgow. We knew all along that that would be a big,big game and that if we won it we would be well on our way to England.

We were based at Troon beforehand and the lads always enjoy that although, as ever, there were hiccups during the build-up. We had the usual spate of call-offs and one unusual one as Andy Goram declared he wasn't 'mentally attuned' for the game. All sorts of stories flew around about that but the only thing I was concerned about was the fact that we had lost a tremendous keeper from the squad. I don't know the ins and outs and I don't really care other than to say it was disappointing. Equally, I was delighted when Andy returned to the fold for the next game against Finland and, believe me, I would love it if he and Jim Leighton are around in England in the summer.

The one bright spot – if you can call it that! – was the return of Ally McCoist after nearly two years out through injury. Typically, the Rangers striker proceeded to steal the show. He was left on the bench at the start mainly because he had hardly kicked a ball in earnest for ages but with the score still 0–0 he was pushed on along with John Robertson in place of Duncan Shearer and Darren Jackson. Even Ally couldn't have predicted what happened next. Within sixty seconds, and with just his second touch, he headed home a great John Collins cross. It was incredible. And Ally, naturally, was off and running over the advertising hoardings and nearly out of Hampden before we got to him.

Later that night the lads were all asking him for his Lottery numbers and telling him he was a jammy so-and-so but really, it isn't just luck with him. He has done it too often – and at crucial moments – for that to be the case. And that was another classic piece of timing because it pushed us to the very edge of qualifying.

Team: Leighton, Burley, McKimmie, Boyd, T. McKinlay, Calderwood, McAllister, McCall, Collins, Shearer, Jackson. Substitutes: McCoist for Shearer, Robertson for Jackson.

Then it was Finland. We were back down at Troon and the biggest talking point beforehand was the prospect of being able to see *Braveheart*, the new Mel Gibson movie. Ally went to the première on the Sunday night before the game, and raved about it so much that the *Daily Record* tried to fix it for us to see it before the game. It was a great idea and I was all for it, but unfortunately we just couldn't fit it into the training schedule.

The only other thing was the surprise we got when the team was announced. We expected Coisty and Scott Booth to be up front, but Craig paired the Aberdeen youngster with John Spencer. Maybe, looking back, I shouldn't have been so surprised, because Spenny looked sensational in training and he had played more football than Ally. But it was Scott who stole the headlines with an early goal that proved to be the winner, and that was more or less us. The boys were jubilant in the dressing-room and there was a real buzz about us because we knew exactly what we had achieved. Craig thanked us all for our efforts and I headed for home, well pleased with life.

Team: Leighton, McKimmie, Boyd, Calderwood, Hendry, T. McKinlay, Spencer, McLaren, Booth, McAllister, Collins. Substitutes: McCoist for Spencer, Jackson for Booth, B. McKinlay for McKimmie.

I know this Scotland squad is not going to lose many goals to anyone anywhere, and that is always the first piece of the jigsaw. That always gives you a chance. Now, as England looms, I believe we have enough competition for places throughout the team to make things all a bit interesting in the finals.

CHAPTER FIFTEEN

Stars in My Eyes

There have been some unbelievable characters – and excellent players – in the Scotland squads I have been part of over the years, and I can't think of anyone I didn't get on with. Some became bigger pals than others, of course, but all in all, I like to think I have made a few good mates from all over the place.

One regret I have, though, is that a lot of the characters have gone out of the scene since I first arrived. In those days you needed eyes in the back of your head and you daren't turn your back on anyone for a second or you'd be done like a dinner in some shape or form. Sometimes it was a nightmare and you wouldn't know which way to turn, but there was never any malice in it and the lads were just clowning around enjoying themselves.

That still goes on but maybe not to the same extent either at club or country level and there's no obvious explanation why not. Maybe players are somehow more 'professional', although I don't think you could label some of the guys I met early on in my international career as unprofessional. After all, the likes of Roy Aitken, Alex McLeish, Davie Cooper and Ally McCoist – to take just a few examples – must have won just about all there is to win. Including, surely, the World Cup for wind-ups! They were always at the capers whether we were in Glasgow or Gothenburg, Turin or Troon.

But, for all the patter, they never lost sight of the real reason why we were together, and you don't win the number of caps those guys did unless you can play a bit. You have to be able to mix it with the best, and those lads – and others – were eminently capable of doing just that in some style. So, really, they deserve their place of honour here, either because they are outstanding players or because they are genuine jokers or because they've managed to combine both things nicely.

Maurice Johnston is another. The wee man is still going strong, and if he had done everything he's meant to have done through his career I think he would have been struggling by now. He's got to be the most maligned player this country has produced in decades. He's been in all sorts of scrapes – some through his own efforts and others because he's maybe been an easy target. But he's good value for all that.

Despite that 'playboy' image, he was – is – a helluva good player. I have always rated Maurice but I think the best times for him were the years he had in France and when he returned to Scotland – controversially as ever – to sign for Rangers. Any time I saw him on TV playing for Nantes, he was absolutely flying. The continental game seemed to suit him down to the ground and he looked a fabulous player. He did unbelievably well at Ibrox, too. I say unbelievably because it can't have been easy for him to go there just a couple of weeks after putting on a Celtic jersey and saying they were the only team he ever wanted to play for! But he did exactly the right thing by giving the 'Gers 110 per cent, and the fact that he scored the winner against the Celts fairly early in his career probably didn't do him any harm.

Apart from that, which will give him a place in Scottish football folklore forever, he should have entered the record books for something else. I still can't quite fathom out how his shot late on in the Scotland game against Brazil in the 1990 World Cup didn't go in. Somehow, the Brazilian keeper Taffarel stopped it, at the same time preventing the Scots from getting the draw that would have taken us to the next stage for the first time. Maurice would have deserved that moment of glory because, despite his somewhat chequered history, I haven't seen many players work harder. He trained like a beast and was a smashing player for Scotland. I hope that's never forgotten when people look at his international career. That somehow happens when a player has been a bit, how shall I put it, controversial.

But one man who will be judged solely on his football merits and nothing else is Paul McStay. The Celtic star has grown up with me since the days when we competed against each other at boys club level, and I have always respected his ability – although, again, some people have never given him the credit he deserves. At club level he has struggled through some difficult times at Parkhead when he, virtually alone, has been the side's saviour. When things have been happening across Glasgow at Ibrox, as they have over the years, it is far too much of a burden to ask one man to carry Rangers' main rivals. Yet Celtic appear to have done that at times, and although Paul happily accepted the role, there is no doubt his form suffered along with the rest.

His lowest moment, I would imagine, was when he missed that crucial Coca-Cola Cup final penalty against Raith Rovers, when it went all the way to the wire. It is a desperate way for any side to lose any game, never mind a cup final, and someone has to be the fall guy. On that occasion it was Paul, and that surely proves just how cruel this game can be – because if anyone *didn't* deserve that recognition it was surely him. He has tried to lead by example through Celtic's lean years – and more often than not he has succeeded. But he was desperately down after that game, and I felt for him because the pressure was enormous. You could tell Paul, and the other Celtic lads like John Collins and Tom Boyd, were badly affected by the final defeat when they joined the Scotland squad soon after. They found it difficult, naturally, to shrug off a loss like that, yet they did it in due course and Paul, for example, went on to play some outstanding football again as the season progressed. He came back incredibly well from that personal anguish and I was thrilled and delighted for him when I saw him lift the Scottish Cup above his head after

Celtic beat Airdrie in that final at the end of the season. You could almost see the strain lift from his shoulders as his beloved club ended their trophy drought. And for Paul it was clearly a special moment. It got that monkey off his – and Celtic's – back and he looked almost as much relieved as he was happy; but I have to say I think he deserved that moment of glory.

Paul has been a terrific player for Celtic for a long time and I have tremendous respect for him. You get to appreciate someone's skill and ability when you play alongside them and I have done that with Paul for Scotland. I have always rated him, but when we play together in the same area of the park I have learned to appreciate him more and more. It frustrates me a bit when I hear or read criticism of him playing in Scotland's colours. But it is probably the same people who criticised Kenny Dalglish for his international efforts, and no one can say he was anything other than a marvellous player. It's just something Paul has had to live with, and he's done that quietly and professionally.

Someone else who has gone about his business professionally – if not exactly quietly – is Ally McCoist. He was actually at Fir Park Boys Club for a spell but they only recognised genuine talent! That's maybe just as well, because imagine being lumbered with listening to Ally all through your career. It's bad enough when we're together on international duty. But I'm not really giving him any stick. He's a nice guy who seems capable of making everyone laugh – even when he's not playing!

I don't think I've ever seen Coisty on a downer, although there must have been moments – maybe in his early struggling days at Ibrox or when he seemed to be constantly on the bench during Graeme Souness's time as manager – when things weren't going his way. If he was, he must have kept his troubles private because any time I saw him he was as chirpy as ever. And, believe me, that's chirpy. Never mind opposing goalkeepers who have to be on their toes when Ally's around, think about his poor teammates. The one thing you can more or less guarantee with Coisty is that he'll have the last word – or at least he'll try to – all the time. It doesn't matter who he's talking to or where he is. I wonder how Her Majesty the Queen got a word in when she presented Ally with his MBE!

I remember when we both played in a testimonial match for Motherwell's John Gahagan. There was a decent crowd at Fir Park but they were all in the stands at the sides of the pitch. No one was in the areas at either end. Well, nearly no one. Behind the goal at one end were two youngsters – obviously Mother-well fans – and what they gave Coisty was something else. They were merciless. They obviously didn't fancy either Ally or Rangers, and it was a non-stop barrage. But Ally being Ally, he eventually scored and, of course, it was right under the noses of the two fans. Honestly, you would have thought he had scored the winning goal in a Cup final against Celtic. He ran about demented as he celebrated, and all the while he gave the two lads some stick in return. They went a bit quiet after that.

Then there was the time in Sweden during the European Championships in the summer of 1992. Ally was probably Scotland's biggest name out there and he got a lot of attention, but that didn't stop us giving him a hard time. There was a guy called Stefan Reuter who played for Germany, and after a game we saw on video when he got a particularly hard time from his opponent and generally had a bit of a nightmare, we used to say that whoever in the Scotland squad was struggling was 'having a Reuter'. It became an expression for whoever was having a disaster and it was good fun. But after a couple of games when Ally, who had been expected to score in the finals, had still failed to notch up a strike, we had to have a change of name. Every day in training thereafter 'having a Reuter' was turned into 'having a Coisty' and poor Ally got a really hard time. But it was only friendly stick and he took it well. At one point he admitted: 'Top scorer here? I haven't even had a shot yet!'

He can take it as well as dish it out and I wouldn't have a word said against him. Mind you, there are times when he has to bow to the inevitable and realise he just can't win. One of those moments was a just a few months ago. I was standing at Faro airport in Portugal waiting for a flight home from my holidays when I felt a tap on the shoulder. I turned round to find Ally right behind me. He was standing there in shorts and a T-shirt looking a bit agitated, like a man in a hurry. It seemed he was due in at Ibrox for the first day of pre-season training that morning! Rangers manager Walter Smith had tracked him down to his holiday villa and gently explained that Ally was due back a few days earlier than the rest because he had been injured. It was certainly enough to put Coisty in a flap. I've thought about that chance meeting since then and I have to say I don't think I've ever seen him move as quickly on the park. I think that return journey was probably a 'flight to hell' for him!

But overall he's not done badly for Rangers. His goals record is phenomenal. He has helped them to a host of honours and has become a hugely popular figure. I've enjoyed teaming up with him in Scotland squads. I'm just glad I don't room with him!

Richard Gough is another Ranger who has always impressed me, either playing with or against him. He was quite magnificent in the European Championship finals in Sweden in 1992, when he came up against some of the best strikers in the world and didn't look at all out of place. And he was brilliant in the Battle of Britain games between Leeds and Rangers. He loves the big-time atmosphere and I think major games like those bring out the best in him. But he has had an enormously successful career generally and he is bound to go down in history as one of the great Ibrox captains. Not that I think for a second he's finishing just yet. One of Richard's greatest strengths is his fitness and I don't know many players who look after their bodies better than he does. He is acutely aware that his body is his bank and, playing at the back as he does, I would expect him to be able to go on at the top level for a while yet. And I can't imagine Rangers rushing to end what has been such an important career for the club.

Other experienced professionals who have done the business for Scotland – and who helped me personally – were guys like Roy Aitken, Alex McLeish and Murdo MacLeod. They have had tremendous international careers and they gave me a lot of good advice at the start of my own Scotland efforts. As well as playing with some style, they all thought a lot about the game and it was clear to me even then that they had picked up and retained good ideas throughout their careers. That's why I'm not really surprised to see the two ex-Celts and Eck are all making their mark at managerial level. It's a relatively new experience for them to be bosses but the way they've started off in that direction suggests they will go on to great things. Remember, you heard it here first!

But if their international careers are over then there are one or two guys I would expect to get theirs under way properly sooner rather than later. One of the names is fairly obvious: Duncan Ferguson. The other, John Spencer, might be more of a surprise.

Dealing with Fergie first, there is no doubt in my mind that he can go on and become a very good player for Scotland. I know he has had his moments on and off the park when he should have taken a step back, counted to at least ten and then got on with things again. But that's easier to do for some people than it is for others and, let's face it, it would be a strange world if we were all made the same way.

Dunc, though, has got to learn not to cross the line between what's acceptable and what's not. I genuinely believe he has made inroads to that, especially since he left Scotland. He's not quite the target in the south that he was at Dundee United and Rangers, and I mean that in both a playing and non-playing sense. He doesn't stick out quite as much in England, and that has helped to take off some of the pressure. But really the bulk of the hard work has to be down to him personally, because there is only so much advice and help others can give. Joe Royle at Goodison Park will, I'm sure, have a calming influence on

Duncan, but the rest is up to him. Somehow, he has to retain his personality but get rid of the moments of madness that have littered his career and cost him so dearly up to now. I certainly wouldn't want him to turn into a robot because he's a great lad to have around the place when the Scotland squad meets up.

When he first joined the international set-up, we soon realised what he was like. We were over in America at the time, and in Dunc's first training session he caused a bit of a stir. You might have thought a young lad in these circumstances would want to make an impression but Fergie is a bit different. He took part in a move we were rehearsing and, after his first touch, he shouted across to Andy Roxburgh who was the boss at the time: 'Sair tae,' he yelled and walked off. 'Sair tae' in English translates into 'sore toe', but rather than call the physio on or say to Andy what was happening, he just shouted across and disappeared from the session! The rest of us looked on bemused but that's just typical Dunc. I don't think you could ever say he was exactly your normal everyday player.

But he's good fun and you always need personalities like him around the place – otherwise things might get a bit boring. So if he can get his act together good and proper I would expect him to become a fixture in the Scotland side. Craig Brown, I know, would love to be able to pen his name into every squad. And it's easy to see why: if you look at his ability alone and forget all his idiosyncrasies, he is a very fine young player. He's tall and therefore he's entitled to be good in the air – although I've seen a few players of that height who somehow manage to jump down the way! I recall Dunc making life extraordinarily difficult for Leeds 'upstairs' in a League game last season, so I've seen at first hand the damage he can do. But defenders up and down the country have been surprised when they've found out, to their cost, that he can play a bit on the deck as well. I've watched him quite closely time and time again, and he knows his way around at ground level as well. He has a very assured touch for such a big man and when he gets up a head of steam he's very difficult to shake off the ball. So one way and another he offers his teammates quite a few options, and that is a tremendous asset in a side playing at the highest level. I must admit I would be delighted if he could sort himself out and become a regular in the international set-up.

Spenny, in some ways, is the same as big Dunc in that he is pure dead gallus. 'Gallus' is a Scottish word that somehow seems to sum up the two of them perfectly. It's a difficult term to define for non-Scots but I suppose cocky, streetwise and brash comes close. They're both very confident individuals, and in Spenny's case he doesn't *think* he's a superstar – he *knows* it! But there's nothing wrong with confidence in your own ability so long as you can back up your words with deeds, and the wee Chelsea striker can do that.

Spenny has done brilliantly in English football since he moved from Rangers, and although some people have questioned his lack of height, it doesn't seem to have stopped him doing the business. I don't know whether or not that might prove to be a handicap at international level because he hasn't really been properly tried and tested in that arena yet. He has a few caps but I would like to see him get more, because defenders at any level never feel particularly comfortable when someone like Spenny is snapping at their heels every second of the ninety minutes. I don't suppose his cause was helped much by his ordering-off against Japan in Hiroshima at the end of last season, but Scotland boss Craig Brown is on record as saying that incident won't make any difference in the future, and I would hope that proves to be the case. It would be more than a bit interesting to see Ferguson and Spencer – a definite case of Little and Large – together up front for Scotland. I don't know how it would work on the field but it would be a riot off it!

Colin Hendry is a lad I've only really got to know since he joined the international squad fairly recently. I've played against him countless times in England and always felt he looked the part, but he has come on in leaps and bounds since he became a

Scotland player, something which has more or less coincided with Blackburn Rovers' rise to prominence. And no one could deny that he has played a huge part in the Ewood Park club's success. After all, the way Kenny Dalglish spent money, if there was someone much better, he would have gone out and got him a long time ago. He has grown in confidence and has done wonderfully well for both Blackburn and Scotland.

Colin and I room together at international level and we get along really well. But the big man has a superstition that must rank right up there among the more unusual in a game littered with people who like to walk out of the tunnel first or last, or put on their right boot before the left, or whatever. Col always has to wash his socks before he plays. Don't ask me why. I've never even attempted to discover the reasons and I'm not sure I want to know! No one minds, because when he plays he does well and is such a tremendous enthusiast that it rubs off on everyone else. But our hotel rooms end up looking more like a doctor's surgery after Col has brought in all his bits and pieces. He's got his own physio's bag full of ointments and this and that. I end up having a wee corner of the room after he's got all his stuff in place!

But, like everyone else in the Scotland squads over the last few decades, he still needs the attentions of Jimmy Steel who has been giving players a rub before games for as long as most folk can remember. He's a legend in the Scotland camp just as he is with Celtic as well. Davie Cooper, because of his Rangers connections, used to give Steely some stick but he got it back as well and those two always had some friendly banter on the go. Jimmy does a marvellous job but he likes to give newcomers a bit of a shock and he's been known to give someone who has joined the squad for the first time a fright when he's been giving them a rub! But he's been terrific for his favourite club and for his country over the years and a Scotland dressing-room without him just wouldn't be the same.

CHAPTER SIXTEEN

Looking to the Future

Gary McAllister of Rangers and Scotland. Now there's an interesting thought. It's certainly an idea that has come and gone over the years with what must, to some people, have seemed like monotonous regularity. There has been speculation about me moving to Ibrox just about every season over the last few years, and I have taken all that as a compliment. After all, I happen to believe that Rangers are the biggest club in Britain – yes, bigger even than Manchester United – so to be linked to them officially or unofficially has been a boost to my confidence. Some of it has, of course, been media hype but there has to my certain knowledge been official interest which was, in turn, rejected out of hand by Leeds United not all that long ago.

I think it all started when Graeme Souness became manager of Rangers and he was seen to be changing the face of the club and, for that matter, of Scottish football. My name cropped up in the newspapers fairly regularly at the time but it's impossible to say with any certainty how much truth there was in the rumours. From my point of view, I suspect Graeme had a hit-list of players he wanted. I heard all the rumours and at the time the impression I got was that he wanted England star Neil Webb first and foremost. Next in line was, ironically, Paul Gascoigne who has ended up there anyway, and third was Trevor Steven who they actually signed. I think I might have been fourth choice. That's the Italian way of doing deals. They set up a pecking order of players they would like and work their way through it until they get someone. Graeme stopped when he reached Trevor.

I was an obvious candidate if for no other reason than the fact that I'm Scottish. With UEFA's three-foreigner rule, that's presumably why just about every season since then the same thing has happened. There was a time more recently when I understand Rangers' chairman David Murray put it on record that he would like to sign me, but that upset a lot of people at Elland Road and it never looked like getting off the ground. And in the midst of all the rumours, counter-rumours and occasional fact, I have obviously never heard directly from the Ibrox club. So it has occasionally been a bit difficult, although overall the speculation has never bothered me.

The 64,000-dollar question, though, has to be: would I fancy a move to Rangers? Let me say right away that I think the signing of Gazza has hit the idea on the head once and for all. But as to whether I would – or wouldn't – have gone, it's a tricky one. If Leeds had accepted a bid from Rangers, and therefore indicated that they would let me leave, then I would have had some long and hard thinking to do.

There are, of course, enormous pluses about the prospect of playing for Rangers. As I say, I believe they are the biggest club in the land. Their support is fantastic and fanatical, they have a quite magnificent stadium, a whole host of outstanding players and they are more or less guaranteed European football every year.

Those are powerful arguments, but there are minuses as well. I enjoyed my time in the top division in Scotland and I don't mean it any disrespect at all but I do consider the Premiership to be stronger. Crowds are bigger – naturally, because of the population – grounds generally are better and the standard is, overall, higher. It is a very good league to play in and I would miss it if I left Elland Road.

But this whole thing depends entirely on circumstances

and also on Leeds wanting rid of me which, as far as I know at the moment, isn't the case. United have been very good for me, just as I hope Gary McAllister has been good for the club. I signed a new contract less than two years ago and it takes me up to 1999 when I will be thirty-four-and-a-half. It is a very good deal and it's given me a lot of security. It was a long-term contract, because in England if your deal expires when you're thirty-three you're entitled to a free transfer. Leeds didn't want that to happen and I was more than happy to agree to a longer agreement. When it does expire, I will be just six months away from a testimonial so the incentive is very much there to keep on playing in the first team and be doing well enough at the time to earn myself another contract.

It will make sure there is no resting on my laurels – not that I was every likely to, because there is still an enormous amount I want to achieve as a Leeds player. I am very ambitious and I know United fans, weaned on the glories of an earlier era, share that ambition. The Leeds players of the Don Revie time regret they didn't win more trophies. They were such an outstanding side they felt they perhaps didn't achieve as much success as they might have. We still have a bit to go before we can be mentioned alongside them, but I don't want regrets. I am desperate, for instance, to win the Premiership again but I would also dearly love to get the FA Cup to Elland Road and to win something in Europe. Greedy? Sure. I loved every minute of our title success, and when your appetite has been whetted you want more of the same. So that's a priority.

The Cup, though, has had me on a diet! I've never done really well in the FA Cup, and at Leicester I don't think I won a tie. That has been frustrating because there's a lot of glamour attached to the final and it's a tremendous showpiece occasion which I would love to be part of.

It's the same with Europe. We had great nights at Elland Road against Stuttgart and Rangers. The atmosphere was electric at those ties and I think midweek Euro nights are always that bit special. They're spicy occasions. We haven't had enough of them at Elland Road so I want a bit more of that action and, as skipper, I can't think of many things better than lifting a European trophy above my head.

So now, in my sixth season with Leeds, I still have plenty to play for. This is actually the longest I've ever been at a club because I spent five years at both Motherwell and Leicester. And I want to keep on trucking. Lads like Gordon Strachan and Davie Cooper kept on playing – and how often have you heard a retired professional say that nothing actually beats playing the game?

So I want to keep going and I hope I get the opportunity to do so. I have looked after myself pretty well, and although you never know what's around the corner, I have the contract with Leeds and I want to do enough to earn a new one when the time comes. Maybe the running power will diminish as the years roll by, but I think Strach and Coop and others have proved that a thorough knowledge of the game isn't bad compensation. You can be a bit more economical with your movement and still be a major player. I certainly don't subscribe to the theory that the minute you hit thirty-four or thirty-five you're past it and should hang up your boots without further delay. That is just nonsense and it's criminal to waste ability if you still have something left to offer. I don't intend, if all things are equal, to make that mistake.

It could be, of course, that I don't operate in the same midfield role I have now. Maybe I will play deeper by then – maybe I will even play a bit deeper sooner rather than later because there is a growing trend, on the continent especially, for one-time midfield men to slot in at the back. Lothar Matthaus did it for Germany with some style and a few Bundesliga clubs, as well as the Italians, Spaniards and French, have utilised guys like that in a role at the back. Scotland boss Craig Brown mentioned the possibility of playing Celtic's Paul McStay in that position, a suggestion that was greeted with a barrowload of criticism. I don't think even Paul fancied it very much. But it wouldn't bother me. If Craig asked me to play behind two markers for Scotland I would do it quite happily. Maybe he'll decide there is a game that he thinks can be won by playing that system, and if he does then I would go along with it. The continental teams who use similar tactics reckon it's a good idea to have someone deep who is a good passer of the ball and who can set things up from the back better than from the middle of the park. I can see the sense in all that although – don't get me wrong – I'm not touting for the role. Alan Hansen had the kind of ability to make it work and many good Premiership judges believe Blackburn's Chris Sutton will eventually be deployed there. I confess I've even tried it myself – for Leicester City reserves – and I felt quite comfortable, although maybe international football might be a bit different! But I would give it a go if that was what was wanted.

There will be a time, of course, when the old legs won't even let me stroll about as a spare man at the back, and when that happens I will be very disappointed even if there's obviously nothing I can do about it. But when I finish I don't want it to be with any regrets – or certainly not many. I have tried to be sensible all through my career and from a financial point of view I have had expert advice over the last decade. It's difficult to over-emphasise how important that is, and I've been lucky with my adviser Jon Holmes. He has guided me the right way and looked after my finances, and I have never squandered money.

Professional players at the top level do make a lot. We are well rewarded and I would expect to be quite well off when I finish playing. There's no point in pretending otherwise because fans and the public in general aren't stupid. I won't be mega-wealthy or anything like that, but because I've been sensible and invested my earnings carefully, I would hope to be in the comfort zone. Maybe I could even stop working altogether, although at this point in time there's really no way of knowing – and, anyway, there is no chance of it happening. I just can't see myself not working for a living.

Apart from anything else, I would want to stay in football after I finish playing. I have a preliminary coaching badge and since football is all I've ever been involved with through my working life, I would want to remain in the game. Coaching appeals to me and I would like to think I have picked up enough and learned enough to be able to pass on some of my experience. Coaching then leads more often than not to management, and I believe I could handle that. I would still be able to be involved in the dressing-room banter that is so much part and parcel of football, and I think when the time comes I would have something to offer as a boss. Gary McAllister, manager of Scotland. That sounds good to me.

Let's face it, you have to have ambitions but the managerial ones are hopefully still a bit away. I have enough on my plate as a player right now and this is a career I don't want to see ending yet.

CHAPTER SEVENTEEN

The McAllister All-Star Select

Every manager in the country would love a chairman who gave him an unlimited budget for players. I'm not even talking Blackburn Rovers supremo Jack Walker here. I mean an elastic amount of money that has no end! That's the cash that was made available to me to pick my Premiership Dream Team. Okay, it's just a fantasy side and considering I'm owner, chairman, manager, coach and, for that matter, ball-boy, money shouldn't really be any object. It wouldn't have needed to be either.

The only constraints I put on myself was not to include any of my present Leeds United teammates because I will fall out with enough people over this without starting on my own doorstep at Elland Road.

This is, of course, every fan's favourite pastime. And since football is all about opinions, I don't for a second expect many supporters – if any! – to agree. But since I'm manager – and since this is my book – no one can really argue.

I'll give you the names first of all, followed by the reasons and the formation.

David Seaman
Denis Irwin
Gary Pallister
Colin Hendry

John Moncur
Graeme Le Saux
John Sheridan
David Batty
Eric Cantona
Alan Shearer
Stan Collymore
Substitutes: John Scales, Darren Anderton, Ian Rush.

A few Englishmen, a couple of Irish lads, a Frenchman and a Scot make up my cosmopolitan side. All are from the Premiership and, I'll tell you what, they can all play.

Let's take a closer look at the names and the reasons they're in this McAllister All-Star Select. I just hope none of them want appearance money!

All the arguments may as well start at the beginning with Seaman as my goalkeeper. I think I can hear the growls coming from Ewood Park already – or is it applause from Highbury? Whatever, I just feel David has a slightly bigger presence about him than Tim Flowers.

To be fair, it was a very difficult choice because the Blackburn keeper had a fantastic season last year and my choice of players has basically been made from that time. And I know people will point the finger at Seaman because of that freak goal he lost in the European Cup Winners Cup final against Real Zaragoza. But that's exactly what it was – a freak – and any keeper can get caught by one of them. David, for me, has the edge. He is very difficult to beat – as are Arsenal – and not many shots get past him.

But I would add one rider to my choice and say that if Andy Goram of Rangers was playing in the Premiership I might have gone for him.

Choosing a goalkeeper was actually the easy bit when I look at the rest of the side. I want my team to play in a fluid formation – a kind of 3-4½-2½, in fact. That means having a couple of markers in the centre of the defence with one man lying spare. And my choice for that role will, I'm sure, surprise a lot of people. John Moncur, though, is a player I have always liked. I've spoken elsewhere about the number of continental sides who have a passer at the back.

John, recognised more as a midfield man, is an excellent passer of the ball and I really believe he would be very comfortable in that role behind the two markers. He has a good range of passes. He can play it short or long and he sees things happening very quickly. He looks to me as if he might have picked up some useful hints from the likes of Glenn Hoddle earlier in his career, and that's no bad thing. He's possibly a bit lightweight in some ways but when you can play it covers a lot of other things and, to me, John can play. He has the kind of quality play I like to see at the back and to have someone like him building play from there would be good.

In front of him would be Gary Pallister and Colin Hendry, two big defenders. Both are good in the air and solid on the ground and they can defend very well. But there is more to both Gary and Col.

The Manchester United man has tremendous anticipation and is a great reader of the game. He somehow sees trouble before it fully develops and manages to nip it in the bud before there is real danger. That is an art in itself, and just because he's not throwing himself about the park making do-or-die tackles doesn't mean he is any less effective. After all, you never saw Alan Hansen break sweat far less anything else, and he wasn't such a bad player.

Big Col is my sole Scot and that's nothing to do with the fact that he's my room-mate on international trips – although heaven only knows what he would have been like if he hadn't made it into my side. I think he has become a tremendous player in recent years and his reputation has grown along the way. He has an amazing exuberance for the game and that enthusiasm, allied to a fair bit of skill, makes him a very good defender. Both he and Gary can use the ball well, and since this is a side that plays football, they would feel quite at home. They would be quite happy to come out of defence with the ball at their feet and that's the way I like to see the game played.

On either side of those three I would have Denis Irwin and Graeme Le Saux, who would probably be more midfield men than defenders. Both go forward a lot when playing with their clubs and countries anyway, and that's what I would be wanting them to do for me.

Denis has the pace to get forward and then back again, which is important just in case he has to help out the other three. But what I really like about him is that his midfield or forward colleagues are almost assured of a good ball. He hits great passes, and that is a big plus in his favour. I also think he would link up well – as he has done before – with John Sheridan. They have done it for the Republic and they would do it again here in this team. On top of all that, don't forget that Denis gets his share of goals with those lethal free-kicks of his.

Graeme, meanwhile, is to my mind one of the most exciting players in the Premiership. I know that sounds unlikely in view of the fact that he is basically a defender, but he's spent a lot of his career much further forward and always looks the part. He's also super-fit and, like Denis, can get up and down the park with no problem; he really covers that whole left-hand side of the pitch very well. And in much the same way as Irwin and Sheridan have a good understanding, so too do Le Saux and Alan Shearer, and Graeme knows just when and where to deliver the ball for his front man.

So to my old teammate at Leeds, David Batty. If ever a player was underestimated, it's him. I played alongside Batts a lot and came to appreciate him a great deal, though. Those who think he is only a grinder should look again, closely, at his contribution to a game. They should look beyond his strength in the tackle and see the ability he has, because he is a very intelligent player and a guy who thinks deeply about the game.

Sure, his greatest asset is probably as a defender who sits and breaks things up when the opposition threaten but he can play as well. He has more skill than many people imagine or appreciate and he was a joy to play alongside. But Batts' main job in this side, which has so many attacking options, would be to hold the middle of the park. That way, I'm sure John Sheridan would have a big influence on everyone around him.

Sheridan is another name that might surprise some people but he doesn't waste many balls and I could see him teaming up well with Eric Cantona. There would be some nice passing movements between them, I'm sure. I've always liked watching John and I think he's maybe a bit underrated as well.

But I don't think anyone underrates Cantona's skill and ability and he would be the 'half' in my 3-4½-2½ formation because he would play just in front of midfield but just behind the front two. In fact, Eric would basically have the freedom of the pitch to go where he wanted to go and roam about causing the opposition as much trouble as he could. I would just let him get on with it and do his own thing because he has the precious ability to be able to make something extraordinary out of nothing. There's no real point in trying to give that kind of player a rigid role; you're looking for that spark of invention, that something different, which can win games. You can't shackle someone like Cantona if you want him to produce the goods. He would be able to do that in my team.

Looking at the make-up of the side so far, I would expect Moncur, Sheridan and Cantona to get things going. They are all passers and they can all go forward with style and purpose. I suspect most of the good things I would want to see would stem from them. They would be the heart of the team.

That just leaves the front two, and they would cost around twenty million pounds! That's washers when you have an open cheque-book. They wouldn't even have any natural wingers to feed them, but the likes of Irwin and Le Saux deliver the ball so well they wouldn't need any.

Stan Collymore would drift slightly right. After his unbelievable season last year it was no surprise Liverpool bought him for the staggering figure of £8.5 million. Honestly, he could turn out to be a bargain even at that. His potential is frightening and, when you see what he's already done to the finest defenders in the country, you have to say the sky is the limit. I think Anfield was the right place for him to go because – with all due respect to Nottingham Forest, where I think manager Frank Clark and the likes of Bryan Roy helped him enormously – he will be surrounded by better players. I actually think Liverpool are on the verge of getting back to where they were not so long ago.

But that's a side issue. Going back to Stan the man, I believe that when he's right on top of his game he is very nearly unplayable. His pace and power is awesome and he has a good touch. He also has a cannon in his right foot which helps a bit!

Despite all this, Alan Shearer, for me, is the best there is in the Premiership. When you think of the competition, that's some claim to make. But, really, he's second to none. I have to confess I'm a bit surprised – and delighted for him – by the way he's come back from an injury that threatened his career. He looks in many ways even stronger than before.

There are so many aspects of his game which I admire that it's difficult to know where to start. He has such a terrific all-round appreciation of the game. He knows when to do it himself and he knows when to bring others in, and he's brilliant at both. When he goes it alone his finishing is undoubtedly explosive. He appears to know where the goal is at all times and that awareness means he barely even looks up before he lets fly. How many goals have you seen him score when he doesn't even appear to be in a scoring position? He succeeds because he always knows exactly where he is in relation to the goal. It's that same awareness that makes it look easy when he involves others. He knows where his teammates are and can pick them out with the minimum of fuss and bother.

Then there is the way he can hold the ball up, which is another great asset for a top-class striker. If someone like Le Saux seeks him out on one of those great runs he makes, he has enough strength and belief to be able to hold off defenders until the cavalry arrives.

Ironically, in view of all that, he probably has still to prove himself at international level. But he'll do that in time I'm sure. I have said for a long period that if Blackburn ever wanted to sell Alan, he would become Britain's first ten-million-pound man. In fact, he just has, because that's what I paid to get him into this side!

I reckon – and again there will be plenty who would argue with me – that Shearer and Cantona are the only two genuinely world-class players in the team. The others are all outstanding professionals but those two are just that little bit better than the rest.

The problem, though, is that there's no room for Ian Rush at the end of it all. I agonised over Rushie and I don't mind admitting it. After all, it's not easy to leave out a player with his track record for goals. In fact, I can't believe I've done it. But I decided the best he can hope for is a place on the bench and to go on if things are a bit tight. The one thing Ian can do, as he has proved countless times over the years, is snatch a goal out of nothing, and that's a handy thing to have in reserve. In the passing, he's the kind of experienced player who can help Collymore enormously.

Joining Rush on the sidelines is Darren Anderton, another player I found difficulty in keeping out of the starting line-up. He has already done well for England; from what I saw of their games last season, he was just about the top man. He is still basically a youngster but I think he will become a great player. I can see him giving my side a bit of width by going on to the right if needed. He's a natural wide man, which the team lacks, so it would be an interesting option to give him a spell.

I needed a defender for cover as well, and that's where John

Scales comes in. He has looked a very good player for Liverpool and is a real quality defender. The attractive thing about John is that he could go on at, say, right back or in the centre of the defence and look equally comfortable in both positions. That alone speaks volumes about his ability.

So that's my fourteen – my fantasy football team – and they are all players who can play. That was vital when I came to choose my squad because I like a side to be able to pass the ball, but at the same time vary it by playing it long if necessary. My lot – I'm beginning to sound like a manager! – could certainly do that.

It's not exactly full of cloggers after all, but that wouldn't bother me. The best midfield I ever saw – Alain Giresse, Jean Tigana and Michel Platini of France – couldn't tackle a fish supper but they were formidable nevertheless. And I think they proved the point I was making earlier that you don't have to be an award-winning tackler to be a player in any position. The Premiership, though, can get a bit physical and that's where the likes of big Col and Batts would hold things together. Basically, I wouldn't have any fears for my team and I'm just glad I have such a generous chairman!

The biggest problem wasn't over how much money I spent getting them altogether, it was over who I left out. The current League is packed with big names and outstanding players and it is one of the most exciting spells I have ever been involved with in England. Every team has quality footballers and some of the players who are missing from my squad still cause me a headache thinking about them. There are other goalkeepers, defenders, midfield men and strikers around the country that any number of people would have in their teams. But I'm over the moon with my selection and I'm just going to take things one game at a time.

Now it's back to Howard Wilkinson, Alex Ferguson, Joe Royle and all the other managers. Their jobs are safe.

CHAPTER EIGHTEEN

The Boss

Some people seem to think Howard Wilkinson has an obsession about fitness, almost to the exclusion of all else. But that is simply not true – unless, of course, you call getting his players fit enough to play through an entire season an obsession. It's just a nonsense to think the gaffer concentrates more on that aspect of football than on others, and it bugs me every time I hear the theory. He *does* consider it important and I must say his methods took me aback when I joined Leeds United from Leicester City, but I believe they have made me a better player who, touch wood, suffers fewer injuries than others because of his routines. I also feel they could lengthen my career. It's no coincidence that former players of the manager's regularly phone him after they have finished and gone into coaching or management and ask him for his views. He must have been doing something right all these years.

When you first face one of his pre-season schedules it can be a bit daunting, I must admit. I discovered in my first few days at Elland Road that I wasn't very fit – either that or the other lads were supermen. The demands made on me at my other clubs and then at Leeds were quite dramatically different. It was a shock to the system and I suffered for a while trying to get used to it. But over the years I have become more and more attuned to his methods and pre-seasons now don't seem quite as daunting as they once were.

It's not just me, of course, because all the other lads have faced the same experience. But I think they all recognise that what he makes us go through in the build-up to a new season isn't so much for his benefit as our own. The expression 'Your body is your bank' has been heard quite frequently in recent years, and it sums things up quite nicely. The manager makes sure you're not short-changed.

There is another general principle, though, which is that players in the modern game appreciate more and more how important it is to be fit. I'm not quite ready yet for a zimmer and a free bus pass, but when I was just starting out in football there were some amazing sights when players returned from their summer breaks for pre-season training. They used to come back in all shapes and sizes from holidays that clearly had involved lots of food and drink – and precious little training. It meant they were playing catch-up as soon as the hard work started again, and several days were wasted.

Now, to be fair, it seems a lot different. Players have come to realise the benefits of keeping their fitness ticking over through the summer weeks and I don't think many professionals at the top level do nothing in terms of physical work between seasons. Really, it's just not worth it. Certainly, at Elland Road, the lads are sensible enough to have done some work so they don't come back and have to start from scratch again.

When we do return, we are faced with a few hard weeks but that's only to be expected. This year, for the first time, we knew what we would be facing from the beginning because the management gave us all a programme that was designed to take us from day one right through to the big kick-off. And it shows without any shadow of a doubt that the gaffer doesn't just dream up ideas as he goes along. Our schedule was carefully prepared with day-to-day routines laid out so we knew exactly what we were about over six or seven weeks.

The first thing we do at Leeds that is out of the ordinary is to return around a week earlier than other clubs. The boss likes us to get a lot of the hard graft under our belts, then have a week off, then restart. Again, it's his particular way of doing pre-season training and, when you look at the fitness of the Leeds players, it's difficult to argue against it.

So even before the torture started we knew what we were in for when we came back from the various parts of the globe we had all been holidaying in. Day one was never going to be much fun because the manager and coaches had mapped out a little tester to see who, if anyone, hadn't kept some form of training going. We had to run for twelve minutes and had to cover two miles. I remember the first year I went to Leeds I couldn't do it. But this year, especially since I had been doing even more work than normal after my groin operation in the middle of May, I felt a lot better. That op was overdue and meant me missing the Scotland trip to Japan and also the European Championship match in the Faroe Islands, but at the same time I wanted to get it over and done with as soon as the domestic season had ended. That way I knew I would be ready for the big European tie with Greece in August and the start of this term. So I ran quite a lot after being given the go-ahead by the specialist and I felt good when Leeds restarted. Good but not great, because there are always a few aches and pains when the serious business starts again.

Days two and three were slightly different to the opening burst because we did two sets of continuous running for forty-five minutes each spell. The runs are mixed with 200 metres, 400 metres and all sorts of distances which are designed to pump the heartbeat up. But in the midst of all that we were working with the ball again and that's what footballers like most. The only day we didn't see a ball was the first one and that's understandable.

On day four the emphasis was on stamina work and we did eight 370-metre runs with sixty seconds between them, and we had to maintain our times in each effort. By the end of the week we were doing five 300-metre runs and four 250s to round off a few hard days before we had the weekend off, as always.

At the start of week two we were still doing a fair bit of running but that quickly eased off and the distances got less and less – which was a part of the programme that the lads appreciated! Coincidentally, we were seeing more and more of the ball and it became a bit more enjoyable because of that.

But what we were all waiting for was games. Some players put up with training, others quite enjoy it but what we all want to do more than anything is play, and the match action couldn't come quick enough. So everyone was delighted when we played Scarborough in a bounce friendly and it let the manager play every professional on the books.

The young lads started the game for two reasons. The first was to give them a piece of the action and the other was to get them to take the sting out of the game. It's not peculiar to Scarborough, and I'm certainly not knocking them, but sometimes in these matches the players from the lower league team are looking to make a name for themselves. They occasionally launch one or two nasty tackles to let the big boys know it's not going to be a picnic, so it's only sensible to let the youngsters get kicked before things settle down! And the kids nowadays can generally look after themselves anyway. We find that out in training ourselves.

But by the end of the game it was more or less the first team who were playing and a match like that served a purpose. It gave us a feel of the action again.

At the beginning of week three we were concentrating mainly on sprints. We did 60-yard and 30-yard runs. In those kind of sessions we did a lot of walking and then went flat out over the 30 or 60 yards and then strolled about for a bit again before repeating the exercise. Day two was still sprinting and we did 3,200 yards of them! They were broken up into six different lengths to vary the routines. But, generally speaking, the hard and long running was over and the ball was more in play with each passing day, so that by the end of that week we were in pretty good nick.

Then the boss does another of these wee things that makes him different to a lot of managers – he gave us a week off. We had started back early so he wanted to break things up a bit and not have us grafting constantly for more than six weeks. So the lads split up again. Tony Yeboah went to Milan for a few days and some of the married lads took their families to Center Parcs, but they all continued some form of training to keep them ticking over. It's a week, really, for quality rest after the serious stuff so nobody overdid it. It was a nice break at a good time and especially for me because I took the opportunity to nip back to Scotland.

I took the chance to go and see my dad and brother but, as it happened, the Open golf championship was on at St Andrews at the same time so I just had to go up there. Pure coincidence, honest. In fact, one person's bad luck was my good fortune because when my old pal Howard Clark failed to make the cut in the tournament I was able to move into his room at the Old Course Hotel. A few of the big-name players were staying there because it's so handy you actually drive over part of the grounds from the famous seventeenth tee. I was in my element. Guys like Bernhard Langer were wandering about, and celebrities like Bruce Forsyth were there as well.

Out on the course I followed Seve Ballesteros – naturally – and also had a look at Scots lads like Sam Torrance, Sandy Lyle and young amateur Gordon Sherry, who had a magnificent couple of weeks at the Old Course and at Carnoustie in the Scottish Open the week previously. These guys are just so good and it's always a pleasure to watch them play. I enjoyed the couple of days up there even though I bumped into that man Ally McCoist again!

Ironically, my mate and I left a little bit early to avoid the traffic since we were heading back to Leeds so we didn't see the dramatic finish. When we left it looked as if John Daly was just about home and dry but when we heard on the car radio that Constantino Rocca had forced a play-off I phoned my old man so he could tape it and we called in to Dad's house to watch it on the way south. My wife Denise was very understanding about that quick trip to the golf because the following Tuesday – two days later – I went to South Africa with United and that same day we moved house!

The South African exercise was an interesting one. Last year we went to Malaysia and a lot of people pointed the finger and said it's ridiculous to go so far just for a couple of games. There are arguments for and against. It is a long way for players who face a lot of travelling through the season anyway. But these trips clearly make the club a lot of money in guarantees and on that occasion the time difference was only an hour so there was no particular problem with jetlag or anything like that.

And I enjoyed it. I wanted to see South Africa because I've never been there and it's not the kind of place you go every week. We were based on the outskirts of Johannesburg and we had a bit of time to see round between training and the two games against Sundowns and Benfica. We didn't venture into the city much but what John Pemberton, David White, Gary Speed and I did manage was a helicopter ride to Sun City and Lost City – a fantastic experience. The pilot was very enthusiastic about everything and wanted to show us all he could on the way there and back. It was like going on safari from the air. We saw rhinos, alligators, baboons . . . you name it. It was an incredible journey to the multi-million-pound developments and a breathtaking way to see the wildlife and the scenery.

Sun City and Lost City? Amazing and astonishing. Lost City has been built in the middle of what seems almost to be a crater. It's a tremendous achievement and well worth a visit if you're lucky enough to get the opportunity. I was delighted I went and I know the rest of the lads were gobsmacked by what they saw as well. I would have hated to go all the way to South

Africa and miss the opportunity of going to the two places that
are walking distance from each other. And on the way back to
Jo'burg the pilot did a few manoeuvres that would have turned
the manager a whiter shade of pale if he had witnessed them! He
took us down into valleys and round creeks. It was a memorable
trip one way and another.

But overall it was very much a working trip and it was
worthwhile. We lost 1–0 to Sundowns to a last-minute goal and
then drew with the Portuguese before losing a sudden-death
penalty shoot-out. It's important, though, not to put too much
emphasis on scorelines in pre-season games, although obviously
we would have preferred to win.

The South Africans are certainly keen on their football. We
played in front of crowds of forty thousand and performed at
Ellis Park, where the rugby World Cup final was played a few
weeks previously. The fans and the players are tremendously
enthusiastic and the team we played knew what they were
about.

It was all very interesting although Ellis Park is definitely
for rugby and not football. Being 6,000 feet above sea level gives
you your moments as well! We had been advised that in a short
visit you don't get too badly affected by the altitude but we
suffered enough to know what it must be like in a longer spell.

After that it was games and more games. We played locally,
in Germany against Bayer Leverkusen and in Dublin as we
wrapped up our pre-season work.

Being fit for the start is the be-all and end-all. The running
is one part of it, the ball work another and the games yet
another. It's a jigsaw in which you hope all the pieces come
together and fit properly when the serious business gets under
way. But, as I think you'll appreciate by now, there's not much
left to chance at Elland Road. The fitness routines are hard but
maybe contrary to public opinion the manager doesn't go
around with a whip! He simply wants his players to be properly
fit and well prepared. There really isn't anything wrong with

that. And anyone who does have an argument should look at the Brazilians. They prepare with tremendous thoroughness and they always look like athletes because they're fit. There's nothing to be ashamed of simply because you copy them or take a leaf out of their book. If it's good enough for the world champions then it's good enough for us. The manager takes some of their ideas on board and mixes them with plenty of his own and the package he comes up with hasn't done anyone any harm – only good. After all, we started the season pretty well so we must all be doing something right.

I think Howard will always have his critics and the biggest, most common criticism about the manager is that he's a bit dour. I think, though, that that's just an impression he wants to give. It does take time to get to know him and I'm still doing that after more than five years at the club, four of them as captain. We have a good working relationship although I suppose it could be even better. But it seems to work fine and, since I'm his next-in-command on the pitch, we discuss things more than most.

I don't want him to think I'm after a rise – not a bad idea, mind you – but he does have a fair bit going for him as a boss. His thoroughness, for example, is legendary and one of the most striking things about his managerial style. Nothing escapes him no matter how big or small a detail it might appear to be. When it comes to Leeds' opposition, he has dossiers on each and every club we're likely to play. He doesn't hand out individual ones as I understand Don Revie used to do with our predecessors at Elland Road, but when it comes down to an actual ninety minutes it's pretty unlikely the other side will be able to surprise us.

Taking that a step further, what we tend to do at training on the Friday before a Saturday game, or in midweek if we have a fixture, is get used to the opposition tactics. The gaffer sorts out the reserves the way our opponents will play and we try out a few things against them.

He is also very aware tactically. He spent years working with England watching how other countries play and he's the kind of manager who, if there's a game on somewhere, wants to be there. Seeing so much football gives you different ideas and he puts them all to good use. He's also quite a statistician and a great one for facts and figures. He likes us to be impressed by them and, invariably, we are.

He constantly sets us targets too. He might look at the start of a season and tell us he wants, say, twenty-six points from the first ten matches, or he'll look at a group of three games and demand nine points. It's the same wherever we are in the League. We could be going for the title or a place in Europe or we could be trying to avoid relegation. It doesn't matter.

He's quite intense that way and he's fairly intense before, during and after matches as well, but I can honestly say that I've never seen him throw a complete wobbler the way he apparently used to when he was with Sheffield Wednesday. The lads have all heard the stories of how cups of tea went flying about the Hillsborough dressing-room if things weren't going well, but he must have matured or something because our tea-set has remained intact! He has his moments at half-time if things aren't going well but generally that comes in the shape of a reminder to players that they might not be doing their jobs the way he wants. The boss does it in front of everyone and names the lads he's not happy with, but it's a case of pointing things out rather than trying to belittle anyone.

At the end, he doesn't hold an immediate inquest into how everything has gone right or wrong – he waits until the Monday. That way, all of us have cooled down and had time to think about the game in question. So nobody says or does anything rash, which can happen in the heat of the moment. But if we have carried passengers he'll still name names and want explanations.

The one thing that can happen to the manager in the heat of the moment is that he can get his phrases a bit mixed up. I remember once after Chris Fairclough had had a particularly outstanding first forty-five minutes while the rest of us hadn't, the manager came in at half-time and, instead of telling us to take a leaf out of Chris's book as he meant, he started on about how the defender was 'leaping like an eagle'. Now, I'm not an expert in birds of prey but I don't think too many eagles leap. But that's just a reminder that he's not absolutely perfect!

What he does do, though, he generally does well and his time with England has made him very cosmopolitan. He speaks a few languages and, although it might not be widely known – or believed because of his dour image – he is a good after-dinner speaker.

He and I don't see each other at all socially, but we do have that solid working relationship you need and, although he's had his ups and downs at Elland Road, he can claim giant successes like the Championship and the First Division title.

The expectations at Leeds are, of course, always massive because of the club's past success, but he is an experienced manager who knows his way around and I would imagine he will stay with the club for a while. He loves putting on a tracksuit and enjoys the day-to-day involvement with the players. We have a good squad of lads and he is very ambitious for us to win things.

The one thing I feel he might do at some point is try his luck as a manager abroad. He's good with languages and I think that ultimately he might quite fancy going continental and working with players who are used to the European way of football. But I suspect there is still quite a lot he wants to achieve with Leeds United before he would consider anything like that.

The Elland Road set-up generally is good. This is a big club from top to bottom and there is an air of professionalism about the place every day of the week. I get involved in a few commercial activities and there are sponsors and such like to speak to whenever it's practical and possible. But clearly most of my time at the club is spent with the manager, coaches and players, and in the summer a couple of new additions were made to the coaching side of things. Mick Hennigan, though, has been with the manager since the pair of them were at Sheffield Wednesday and they are an interesting duo. They would appear to be chalk and cheese but the partnership works and, indeed, maybe that's the secret. Mick is an unbelievable character. He's an out-and-out Yorkshireman and a big Arthur Scargill fan who keeps things boiling around the place. He has fantastic energy and a burning desire to do well so he never lets up and his enthusiasm is infectious.

But there were those interesting additions to the backroom team during the summer who I'm sure will help the club enormously. Howard brought Dave Williams, Paul Hart and Eddie Gray to Elland Road to help behind the scenes. It's an interesting mix of people and personalities who between them have a wealth of experience.

Dave has been schooled in the Norwich way of things which means he likes to see good football. He wants the ball passed about the park neatly and precisely and he has a good pedigree.

The other two, of course, are already well known in and around the club. Paul has been brought in to help the squad's defenders first and foremost I think. He was a fine player himself, and if he can use his experience to turn our lads into better players then everyone will be delighted.

It's the same with Eddie, who is working with the youngsters but also helps out with the first team from time to time. His area is the middle to front players and, again, with the experience he picked up playing so brilliantly for Leeds and Scotland, it would be foolish to think he can't teach us a thing or two. And, let's face it, you never stop learning in football. If you think you know it all you're finished. Vastly experienced professionals like Eddie and Gordon Strachan were learning all the time through their careers and are still doing so now. Strach is using that knowledge at Coventry but he'll still be gathering bits and pieces from people like Ron Atkinson.

Younger players would be half-wits not to listen to these kind of men and I was interested to read in Scotland a couple of months ago that Steven Pressley, the country's Under-21 captain, has been speaking highly of the wee man. 'Elvis' had a spell with Coventry after he left Rangers and before he returned to Scotland with Dundee United and he admitted Strach had been brilliant for him.

But Gordon would be the first to admit there's still time to pick up new, useful information for him as well and Eddie Gray, Howard Wilkinson and plenty of others would agree you're never really the finished article.

I know I'm not.